MASTER THE™ DSST®

Principles of Supervision Exam

About Peterson's

Peterson's® has been your trusted educational publisher for over 50 years. It's a milestone we're quite proud of, as we continue to offer the most accurate, dependable, high-quality educational content in the field, providing you with everything you need to succeed. No matter where you are on your academic or professional path, you can rely on Peterson's for its books, online information, expert test-prep tools, the most up-to-date education exploration data, and the highest quality career success resources—everything you need to achieve your education goals. For our complete line of products, visit **www.petersons.com.**

For more information, contact Peterson's, 4380 S. Syracuse Street, Suite 200, Denver CO 80237; 800-338-3282 Ext. 54229; or find us online at **www.petersons.com**.

ISBN: 978-0-7689-4472-3

Printed in the United States of America

10 9 8 7 6 5 4 3 2 1   23   22   21

Contents

Before You Begin

HOW THIS BOOK IS ORGANIZED

Peterson's *Master the™ DSST® Principles of Supervision Exam* provides a diagnostic test, subject-matter review, and a post-test.

- **Diagnostic Test**—Twenty multiple-choice questions, followed by an answer key with detailed answer explanations
- **Assessment Grid**—A chart designed to help you identify areas that you need to focus on based on your test results
- **Subject-Matter Review**—General overview of the exam subject, followed by a review of the relevant topics and terminology covered on the exam
- **Post-test**—Sixty multiple-choice questions, followed by an answer key and detailed answer explanations

The purpose of the diagnostic test is to help you figure out what you know—or don't know. The twenty multiple-choice questions are similar to the ones found on the DSST exam, and they should provide you with a good idea of what to expect. Once you take the diagnostic test, check your answers to see how you did. Included with each correct answer is a brief explanation regarding why a specific answer is correct, and in many cases, why other options are incorrect. Use the assessment grid to identify the questions you miss so that you can spend more time reviewing that information later. As with any exam, knowing your weak spots greatly improves your chances of success.

Following the diagnostic test is a subject-matter review. The review summarizes the various topics covered on the DSST exam. Key terms are defined; important concepts are explained; and when appropriate, examples are provided. As you read the review, some of the information may seem familiar while other information may seem foreign. Again, take note of the unfamiliar because that will most likely cause you problems on the actual exam.

After studying the subject-matter review, you should be ready for the post-test. The post-test contains sixty multiple-choice items, and it will serve as a dry run for the real DSST exam. There are complete answer explanations at the end of the test.

OTHER DSST® PRODUCTS BY PETERSON'S

Books, flashcards, practice tests, and videos available online at **www.petersons.com/testprep/dsst**

- A History of the Vietnam War
- Art of the Western World
- Astronomy
- Business Mathematics
- Business Ethics and Society
- Civil War and Reconstruction
- Computing and Information Technology
- Criminal Justice
- Environmental Science
- Ethics in America
- Ethics in Technology
- Foundations of Education
- Fundamentals of College Algebra
- Fundamentals of Counseling
- Fundamentals of Cybersecurity
- General Anthropology
- Health and Human Development
- History of the Soviet Union
- Human Resource Management

- Introduction to Business
- Introduction to Geography
- Introduction to Geology
- Introduction to Law Enforcement
- Introduction to World Religions
- Lifespan Developmental Psychology
- Math for Liberal Arts
- Management Information Systems
- Money and Banking
- Organizational Behavior
- Personal Finance
- Principles of Advanced English Composition
- Principles of Finance
- Principles of Public Speaking
- Principles of Statistics
- Principles of Supervision
- Substance Abuse
- Technical Writing

Like what you see? Get unlimited access to Peterson's full catalog of DSST practice tests, instructional videos, flashcards, and more for **75% off the first month!** Go to **www.petersons.com/testprep/dsst** and use coupon code **DSST2020** at checkout. Offer expires July 1, 2021.

Chapter 1

All About the DSST® Exam

WHAT IS DSST®?

Previously known as the DANTES Subject Standardized Tests, the DSST program provides the opportunity for individuals to earn college credit for what they have learned outside of the traditional classroom. Accepted or administered at more than 1,900 colleges and universities nationwide and approved by the American Council on Education (ACE), the DSST program enables individuals to use the knowledge they have acquired outside the classroom to accomplish their educational and professional goals.

WHY TAKE A DSST® EXAM?

DSST exams offer a way for you to save both time and money in your quest for a college education. Why enroll in a college course in a subject you already understand? For more than 30 years, the DSST program has offered the perfect solution for individuals who are knowledgeable in a specific subject and want to save both time and money. A passing score on a DSST exam provides physical evidence to universities of proficiency in a specific subject. More than 1,900 accredited and respected colleges and universities across the nation award undergraduate credit for passing scores on DSST exams. With the DSST program, individuals can shave months off the time it takes to earn a degree.

The DSST program offers numerous advantages for individuals in all stages of their educational development:

- Adult learners
- College students
- Military personnel

Adult learners desiring college degrees face unique circumstances—demanding work schedules, family responsibilities, and tight budgets.

1

Yet adult learners also have years of valuable work experience that can frequently be applied toward a degree through the DSST program. For example, adult learners with on-the-job experience in business and management might be able to skip the Business 101 courses if they earn passing marks on DSST exams such as Introduction to Business and Principles of Supervision.

Adult learners can put their prior learning into action and move forward with more advanced course work. Adults who have never enrolled in a college course may feel a little uncertain about their abilities. If this describes your situation, then sign up for a DSST exam and see how you do. A passing score may be the boost you need to realize your dream of earning a degree. With family and work commitments, adult learners often feel they lack the time to attend college. The DSST program provides adult learners with the unique opportunity to work toward college degrees without the time constraints of semester-long course work. DSST exams take two hours or less to complete. In one weekend, you could earn credit for multiple college courses.

The DSST exams also benefit students who are already enrolled in a college or university. With college tuition costs on the rise, most students face financial challenges. The fee for each DSST exam starts at $85 (plus administration fees charged by some testing facilities)—significantly less than the $750 average cost of a 3-hour college class. Maximize tuition assistance by taking DSST exams for introductory or mandatory course work. Once you earn a passing score on a DSST exam, you are free to move on to higher-level course work in that subject matter, take desired electives, or focus on courses in a chosen major.

Not only do college students and adult learners profit from DSST exams, but military personnel reap the benefits as well. If you are a member of the armed services at home or abroad, you can initiate your post-military career by taking DSST exams in areas with which you have experience. Military personnel can gain credit anywhere in the world, thanks to the fact that almost all of the tests are available through the internet at designated testing locations. DSST testing facilities are located at more than 500 military installations, so service members on active duty can get a jump-start on a post-military career with the DSST program. As an additional incentive, DANTES (Defense Activity for Non-Traditional Education Support) provides funding for DSST test fees for eligible members of the military.

More than 30 subject-matter tests are available in the fields of Business, Humanities, Math, Physical Science, Social Sciences, and Technology.

Available DSST® Exams

Business	Social Sciences
Business Ethics and Society	A History of the Vietnam War
Business Mathematics	Art of the Western World
Computing and Information Technology	Criminal Justice
Human Resource Management	Foundations of Education
Introduction to Business	Fundamentals of Counseling
Management Information Systems	General Anthropology
Money and Banking	History of the Soviet Union
Organizational Behavior	Introduction to Geography
Personal Finance	Introduction to Law Enforcement
Principles of Finance	Lifespan Developmental Psychology
Principles of Supervision	Substance Abuse
	The Civil War and Reconstruction
Humanities	**Physical Sciences**
Ethics in America	Astronomy
Introduction to World Religions	Environmental Science
Principles of Advanced English	Health and Human Development
Composition	Introduction to Geology
Principles of Public Speaking	
Math	**Technology**
Fundamentals of College Algebra	Ethics in Technology
Math for Liberal Arts	Fundamentals of Cybersecurity
Principles of Statistics	Technical Writing

As you can see from the table, the DSST program covers a wide variety of subjects. However, it is important to ask two questions before registering for a DSST exam.

1. Which universities or colleges award credit for passing DSST exams?
2. Which DSST exams are the most relevant to my desired degree and my experience?

Knowing which universities offer DSST credit is important. In all likelihood, a college in your area awards credit for DSST exams, but find out before taking an exam by contacting the university directly. Then review the list of DSST exams to determine which ones are most relevant to the degree you are seeking and to your base of knowledge. Schedule an appointment with your college adviser to determine which exams best fit your degree program and which college courses the DSST exams can replace. Advisers should also be able to tell you the minimum score required on the DSST exam to receive university credit.

DSST® TEST CENTERS

You can find DSST testing locations in community colleges and universities across the country. Check the DSST website (**www.getcollegecredit. com**) for a location near you or contact your local college or university to find out if the school administers DSST exams. Keep in mind that some universities and colleges administer DSST exams only to enrolled students. DSST testing is available to men and women in the armed services at more than 500 military installations around the world.

HOW TO REGISTER FOR A DSST® EXAM

Once you have located a nearby DSST testing facility, you need to contact the testing center to find out the exam administration schedule. Many centers are set up to administer tests via the internet, while others use printed materials. Almost all DSST exams are available as online tests, but the method used depends on the testing center. The cost for each DSST exam starts at $85, and many testing locations charge a fee to cover their costs for administering the tests. Credit cards are the only accepted payment method for taking online DSST exams. Credit card, certified check, and money order are acceptable payment methods for paper-and-pencil tests.

Test takers are allotted two score reports—one mailed to them and another mailed to a designated college or university, if requested. Online tests generate unofficial scores at the end of the test session, while individuals taking paper tests must wait four to six weeks for score reports.

PREPARING FOR A DSST® EXAM

Even though you are knowledgeable in a certain subject matter, you should still prepare for the test to ensure you achieve the highest score possible. The first step in studying for a DSST exam is to find out what will be on the specific test you have chosen. Information regarding test content is located on the DSST fact sheets, which can be downloaded at no cost from **www.getcollegecredit.com**. Each fact sheet outlines the topics covered on a subject-matter test, as well as the approximate percentage assigned to each topic. For example, questions on the Principles of Supervision exam are distributed in the following way: Roles and Responsibilities of Managers and Supervisors—20%, Management Functions—15%, and Organizational Environment—30%.

In addition to the breakdown of topics on a DSST exam, the fact sheet also lists recommended reference materials. If you do not own the recommended books, then check college bookstores. Avoid paying high prices for new textbooks by looking online for used textbooks. Don't panic if you are unable to locate a specific textbook listed on the fact sheet; the textbooks are merely recommendations. Instead, search for comparable books used in university courses on the specific subject. Current editions are ideal, and it is a good idea to use at least two references when studying for a DSST exam. Of course, the subject matter provided in this book will be a sufficient review for most test takers. However, if you need additional information, then it is a good idea to have some of the reference materials at your disposal when preparing for a DSST exam.

Fact sheets include other useful information in addition to a list of reference materials and topics. Each fact sheet includes subject-specific sample questions like those you will encounter on the DSST exam. The sample questions provide an idea of the types of questions you can expect on the exam. Test questions are multiple-choice with one correct answer and three incorrect choices.

The fact sheet also includes information about the number of credit hours ACE has recommended be awarded by colleges for a passing DSST exam score. However, you should keep in mind that not all universities and colleges adhere to the ACE recommendation for DSST credit hours. Some institutions require DSST exam scores higher than the minimum score recommended by ACE. Once you have acquired appropriate reference materials and you have the outline provided on the fact sheet, you are ready to start studying, which is where this book can help.

TEST DAY

After reviewing the material and taking practice tests, you are finally ready to take your DSST exam. Follow these tips for a successful test day experience.

1. **Arrive on time.** Not only is it courteous to arrive on time to the DSST testing facility, but it also allows plenty of time for you to take care of check-in procedures and settle into your surroundings.
2. **Bring identification.** DSST test facilities require that candidates bring a valid government-issued identification card with a current photo and signature. Acceptable forms of identification include a current driver's license, passport, military identification card, or state-issued identification card. Individuals who fail to bring proper identification to the DSST testing facility will not be allowed to take an exam.
3. **Bring the right supplies.** If your exam requires the use of a calculator, you may bring a calculator that meets the specifications. For paper-based exams, you may also bring No. 2 pencils with an eraser and black ballpoint pens. Regardless of the exam methodology, you are NOT allowed to bring reference or study materials, scratch paper, or electronics such as cell phones, personal handheld devices, cameras, alarm wrist watches, or tape recorders to the testing center.
4. **Take the test.** During the exam, take the time to read each question-and-answer option carefully. Eliminate the choices you know are incorrect to narrow the number of potential answers. If a question completely stumps you, take an educated guess and move on—remember that DSSTs are timed; you will have 2 hours to take the exam.

With the proper preparation, DSST exams will save you both time and money. So join the thousands of people who have already reaped the benefits of DSST exams and move closer than ever to your college degree.

PRINCIPLES OF SUPERVISION EXAM FACTS

The DSST® Principles of Supervision exam consists of 100 multiple-choice questions that cover the basics of managerial and supervisory skills, challenges, and responsibilities. The exam focuses upon the list of topics below. Careful reading, critical thinking, and logical analysis will be as important as your knowledge of management and supervision.

Area or Course Equivalent: Principles of Supervision
Level: Lower-level baccalaureate
Amount of Credit: 3 Semester Hours
Minimum Score: 400
Source: https://www.getcollegecredit.com/wp-content/assets/
factsheets/PrinciplesOfSupervision.pdf

Below is an outline of what you can expect to be covered on the exam.

I. Roles and Responsibilities of Managers and Supervisors—20%

    a. Evolution of management/supervision

    b. Knowledge and skill requirements

    c. Managerial roles

    d. Levels of management

    e. Business ethics and corporate social responsibility

II. Management Functions—50%

    a. Planning

    b. Organizing and staffing

    c. Leading

    d. Controlling

III. Organizational Environment—30%

    a. Legal, political, economic, and social

    b. Labor-management relations (unions vs. non-unions, exempt vs. non-exempt)

    c. Organizational culture

    d. Diversity and inclusion

    e. Global

    f. Sustainable environments

    g. Organizational change

    h. Workplace safety and security

Chapter 2

Principles of Supervision Diagnostic Test

DIAGNOSTIC TEST ANSWER SHEET

1. Ⓐ Ⓑ Ⓒ Ⓓ   8. Ⓐ Ⓑ Ⓒ Ⓓ   15. Ⓐ Ⓑ Ⓒ Ⓓ

2. Ⓐ Ⓑ Ⓒ Ⓓ   9. Ⓐ Ⓑ Ⓒ Ⓓ   16. Ⓐ Ⓑ Ⓒ Ⓓ

3. Ⓐ Ⓑ Ⓒ Ⓓ   10. Ⓐ Ⓑ Ⓒ Ⓓ   17. Ⓐ Ⓑ Ⓒ Ⓓ

4. Ⓐ Ⓑ Ⓒ Ⓓ   11. Ⓐ Ⓑ Ⓒ Ⓓ   18. Ⓐ Ⓑ Ⓒ Ⓓ

5. Ⓐ Ⓑ Ⓒ Ⓓ   12. Ⓐ Ⓑ Ⓒ Ⓓ   19. Ⓐ Ⓑ Ⓒ Ⓓ

6. Ⓐ Ⓑ Ⓒ Ⓓ   13. Ⓐ Ⓑ Ⓒ Ⓓ   20. Ⓐ Ⓑ Ⓒ Ⓓ

7. Ⓐ Ⓑ Ⓒ Ⓓ   14. Ⓐ Ⓑ Ⓒ Ⓓ

PRINCIPLES OF SUPERVISION DIAGNOSTIC TEST
24 minutes—20 questions

Directions: Carefully read each of the following 20 questions. Choose the best answer to each question and fill in the corresponding circle on the answer sheet. The Answer Key and Explanations can be found following this Diagnostic Test.

1. Which of the following is NOT a twenty-first century global challenge faced by business management?

   A. International trade agreements
   B. Exchange rates
   C. Cultural environments
   D. Organizational size

2. Who of the following is in daily contact with blue-collar workers in an organization?

   A. Middle-level manager
   B. Tactical manager
   C. Operational manager
   D. Strategic manager

3. Which of the following is on the highest level of Maslow's hierarchy of needs?

   A. Shelter
   B. Achievement
   C. Security
   D. Friendship

4. The management process used to compare actual performance to organizational goals is known as

   A. produce.
   B. inspect.
   C. control.
   D. plan.

5. Which of the following terms is commonly used to refer to the system of behavior and rituals that distinguishes one company from another in the same industry?

   A. Organization
   B. Environment
   C. Society
   D. Culture

6. Which of the following focuses on short-term goals of an organization?

   A. Strategic planning
   B. Control planning
   C. Operational planning
   D. Tactical planning

7. The addition of a new product or the removal of an existing product to a company's product line are examples of

   A. organization-wide changes.
   B. transformational changes.
   C. subsystem changes.
   D. remedial changes.

8. The ability of a manager to diagnose and solve problems is a function of

   A. people skills.
   B. computer skills.
   C. analytical skills.
   D. conceptual skills.

9. Which of the following terms is commonly used to refer to the process of assigning tasks to subordinates?

   A. Delegation
   B. Accountability
   C. Authority
   D. Responsibility

10. All of the following exert a direct and immediate influence upon the daily activities of a business EXCEPT:

    A. Competitor pricing
    B. Customer spending
    C. Raw material quality
    D. Population shifts

11. Setting goals for employees and closely supervising quality and accuracy are behaviors that describe

    A. transformational leadership.
    B. charismatic leadership.
    C. group maintenance leadership.
    D. task performance leadership.

12. The ten roles of managers were first identified by

    A. Carly Fiorina.
    B. Henry Mintzberg.
    C. Rensis Likert.
    D. Abraham Maslow.

13. Directing and monitoring ongoing activities during production at a factory are typical of

    A. clan control.
    B. feedback control.
    C. concurrent control.
    D. feedforward control.

14. A person who buys four pairs of shoes at an outlet mall is best described as a(n)

    A. intermediate consumer.
    B. wholesale consumer.
    C. mass consumer.
    D. final consumer.

15. Which of the following methods of departmentalization is most likely to trigger confusion regarding authority?

    A. Product organization
    B. Matrix organization
    C. Customer organization
    D. Functional organization

16. The Sarbanes-Oxley Act was enacted in response to

   A. corporate accounting scandals.
   B. age discrimination lawsuits.
   C. sexual harassment complaints.
   D. hazardous waste disposal.

17. Which of the following serves as a benchmark for performance assessment?

   A. Reward
   B. Standard
   C. Vision
   D. Expectancy

18. General influences on a business, such as regulatory agencies and global markets, are known as the

   A. competitive environment.
   B. macro environment.
   C. internal environment.
   D. microenvironment.

19. Which of the following is NOT one of the four established functions of management?

   A. Evaluating
   B. Leading
   C. Planning
   D. Controlling

20. A leader who has a personality that employees find admirable is most likely using

   A. expert power.
   B. coercive power.
   C. referent power.
   D. legitimate power.

ANSWER KEY AND EXPLANATIONS

1. D	5. D	9. A	13. C	17. B
2. C	6. C	10. D	14. D	18. B
3. B	7. C	11. D	15. B	19. A
4. C	8. C	12. B	16. A	20. C

1. **The correct answer is D.** Organizational size was at one time a challenge faced by business management striving to stay competitive, but global factors have changed the business landscape. Technology has made competition fiercer, and choices A, B, and C are all factors that impact a business's ability to compete globally.

2. **The correct answer is C.** Frontline or operational managers are in daily contact with the workers in an organization. Middle-level managers (choice A) and tactical managers (choice B) are synonymous, and they are the link between top-level managers and frontline managers. Strategic managers, or top-level managers (choice D), are responsible for long-term planning rather than daily operations.

3. **The correct answer is B.** Achievement falls in the category of esteem, which is near the top of Maslow's hierarchy of needs. Shelter (choice A) is a physiological need at the bottom, followed by security (choice C). Friendship (choice D) is an element of social needs, which are beneath esteem and self-actualization.

4. **The correct answer is C.** The control process is a management function used to compare actual performance with organizational goals and standards. Choices A and B don't make sense. While controlling and planning are two closely connected management functions, choice D is incorrect because planning directs the way in which managers organize, lead, and control.

5. **The correct answer is D.** *Organizational culture* is the term used to refer to the system of behavior and rituals that distinguish one company from another. Managers define the culture of a business through employee training, motivational methods, and behavioral expectations. Choices A, B, and C are not terms that describe the goals and practices shared by employees of a company.

6. **The correct answer is C.** Operational planning focuses on the short-term plans of an organization, which are typically less than two years. Strategic planning (choice A) relates to long-term goals, control planning (choice B) is not one of the three levels of planning, and tactical planning (choice D) involves intermediate-term goals.

7. **The correct answer is C.** Subsystem changes include the addition of a new product or the removal of an existing product from a company's product line. Subsystem changes can also include departmental reorganizations. In contrast, organization-wide changes (choice A) involve the entire company and can include major restructuring, significant layoffs, or significant staff additions. Transformational changes (choice B) are radical, such as the reorganization of a company's entire management team and reporting hierarchy. Remedial changes (choice D) are implemented to remedy an issue such as poor product performance.

8. **The correct answer is C.** Analytical skills refer to a manager's ability to diagnose and solve problems. A manager with good people skills (choice A) works well with others. Computer skills (choice B) refer to a manager's ability to use business software to maximize job performance. Conceptual skills (choice D) involve seeing the big picture and developing long-range plans.

9. **The correct answer is A.** Delegation involves assigning tasks or responsibilities to subordinates. Accountability (choice B) is the expectation that a worker will complete a task or face consequences. Authority (choice C) is the power to make a decision. Responsibility (choice D) refers to an employee's obligation to carry out an assigned task.

10. **The correct answer is D.** A population shift is an indirect force on a business that has long-term effects. Competitors, customers, and suppliers are direct forces on an organization that have immediate and daily effects. The price of a competitor's product influences consumer spending, and the quality of raw materials provided by a supplier affects the quality of a product made by a business.

11. **The correct answer is D.** Goal setting and close supervision characterize task performance leadership. Transformational leaders (choice A) motivate others to focus on the good of the group. Charismatic leaders (choice B) arouse excitement in followers. Group maintenance leaders (choice C) focus on group stability and harmony.

12. **The correct answer is B.** Henry Mintzberg is an academic who conducted research about management roles. Carly Fiorina (choice A) is the former CEO of Hewlett-Packard. Rensis Likert (choice C) researched management styles and developed the linking pin model. Abraham Maslow (choice D) developed the theory of a hierarchy of needs.

13. **The correct answer is C.** Concurrent control focuses on directing, monitoring, and modifying ongoing activities related to any type of business operation. Clan control (choice A) is not typically used to manage specific tasks like manufacturing. Feedback control (choice B) takes place before activities begin. Feedforward control (choice D) evaluates results.

14. **The correct answer is D.** Final consumers purchase products or services in their completed form. Intermediate consumers (choice A) buy raw materials from wholesalers to make products to sell to final consumers. Wholesale and mass consumers (choices B and C) are not terms related to consumer types that are a direct environmental force on organizations.

15. **The correct answer is B.** The Matrix organization is most likely to cause employees confusion regarding who is in charge because of its dual line of command. Matrix organization is a blending of product and functional organization (choices A and D). Customer organization (choice C) serves the customers' needs.

16. **The correct answer is A.** The Sarbanes-Oxley Act was enacted in 2002 in response to corporate accounting scandals at Enron and WorldCom. The law established strict accounting rules that make top-level managers more responsible for violations. The Sarbanes-Oxley Act does not address age discrimination lawsuits (choice B), sexual harassment complaints (choice C), or hazardous waste disposal (choice D).

17. **The correct answer is B.** Standards serve as benchmarks for performance assessments and clarify desired performance levels. In the control function, the first step involves setting performance standards based on quantity, quality, time, and cost. Rewards (choice A), visions (choice C), and expectancies (choice D) do not serve as performance assessment benchmarks.

18. **The correct answer is B.** Macro environment refers to general influences on a business, which are also known as indirect forces. Indirect forces include laws, economies, technological advancements, and global markets. A competitive environment (choice A) refers to direct forces, such as suppliers and customers. The internal environment (choice C) of an organization is its employees, management style, and organizational culture. A microenvironment (choice D) is the opposite of a macro environment.

19. **The correct answer is A.** The four functions of management as developed by Henri Fayol are planning, organizing, leading, and controlling. Evaluating is not one of the specified functions, although evaluation occurs in the organizing stage.

20. **The correct answer is C.** A leader with a personality that employees find admirable is using referent power. Expert power (choice A) refers to a leader's experience. A leader with coercive power (choice B) controls punishments that employees want to avoid. Legitimate power (choice D) is the authority to tell subordinates what to do.

DIAGNOSTIC TEST ASSESSMENT GRID

Now that you've completed the diagnostic test and read through the answer explanations, you can use your results to target your studying. Find the question numbers from the diagnostic test that you answered incorrectly and highlight or circle them below. Then focus extra attention on the sections within the chapter dealing with those topics.

Principles of Supervision		
Content Area	**Topic**	**Question #**
Roles and Responsibilities of Managers and Supervisors	• Evolution of management/supervision • Knowledge and skill requirements • Managerial roles • Levels of management • Business ethics and corporate social responsibility	2, 8, 12, 16
Management Functions	• Planning • Organizing and staffing • Leading • Controlling	3, 4, 6, 9, 11, 13, 15, 17, 19, 20
Organizational Environment	• Legal, political, economic, and social • Labor-management relations (e.g., union vs. non-union, exempt vs. nonexempt) • Organizational culture • Diversity and inclusion • Global • Sustainable environments • Organizational change • Workplace safety and security	1, 5, 7, 10, 14, 18

Chapter 3

Principles of Supervision Subject Review

OVERVIEW
- **Roles and Responsibilities of Managers and Supervisors**
- **Management Functions**
- **Organizational Environment**
- **Summing It Up**

ROLES AND RESPONSIBILITIES OF MANAGERS AND SUPERVISORS

Effective managers and supervisors facilitate the activities within organizations through planning, organizing, leading, and controlling. This involves understanding the basics of the roles and responsibilities associated with these positions as well as employing the principles of supervision. The best managers and supervisors use the principles to guide the work of others and help organizations meet short-term needs and accomplish long-term goals.

....

TIP: The purpose, norms, and values of an organization trickle down from top-level managers.

....

The Evolution of Management and Supervision

Modern management could be said to have begun with the **industrial revolution**. Prior to that, there were only a few entities large and sophisticated enough to require the kinds of planning, control, and resource allocation associated with management: the Church; armies and navies, and the governments which sponsored them; and large agricultural enterprises requiring that someone manage the workers and processes peculiar to agriculture. But prior to the industrial revolution—which would come to directly influence agricultural practices, including planting, harvesting, and the division of labor responsible for those—not even the largest of farms and plantations were home to anything resembling modern management.

The Industrial Revolution & Scientific Management

The industrial revolution allowed production at a scale never seen before, and the owners of the new, larger enterprises were no longer able to efficiently oversee large operations that required layers of control in order to efficiently mass produce goods. Production at that scale required unheard of levels of quality control, specialization of labor, standardized processes, accounting, and workflow planning.

The industrial revolution made almost inevitable the idea that organizations themselves could be considered machines in their own right: the idea that management was itself a discipline that could be studied, measured, and improved upon naturally followed.

The best known proponent of this sort of **"scientific management"** was Frederick Taylor, who argued in the early 1900s that businesses should be run in a scientific, efficient manner. He felt that the scientific method, applied to the management of business, would result in businesses that outperformed earlier institutions run by brilliant (but unscientific) "captains of industry." Taylor sought the one "best" practice that would lead to optimum performance, and to arrive at that optimum, he sought to break down complex tasks into easily repeatable subtasks the performance (and output) of which could be accurately measured.

Taylor's scientific management was in effect a **mechanistic** view that tended to regard employees as replaceable cogs in the business "machine," and critics have charged that, while the approach did increase production, it also resulted in the dehumanization of workers.

Social Science & Bureaucratic Management

By the 1950s, social scientists, including sociologist and economist **Max Weber**, showed that insights from such disciplines as psychology and sociology could be brought to bear on theories of management. At the same time, writers such as Peter Drucker, in *Concept of the Corporation* (1946), began exploring the idea that *knowledge* was itself a valuable commodity. Information was of value not only in and of itself, said Drucker, but also because information—and tools that allowed workers to acquire and share information—made workers and managers more effective and efficient. Information, noted Drucker and others, creates value over and above the exchange of goods and services that were traditionally a company's products. Also, it became obvious that information itself could in fact *be* a product, and what came to be called "knowledge work" quickly became a much larger proportion of the economy.

Weber is often thought of as a fan of large, impersonal bureaucracies, which is an oversimplification. He felt that a well-organized bureaucracy could indeed be efficient, but cautioned against excessively large bureaucracies, noting that in one, a worker begins to feel like a little cog in a machine, and thus becomes overly preoccupied with the idea of becoming, as Weber put it, "a bigger cog."

Theory X and Theory Y: The Human Relations Movement

Much valuable information resides in the heads of employees, so a great deal of value or potential value walks out of the door every evening—and may never return. This important realization led to a school of thought where employees should be treated as important assets; a great deal of a company's capital resides in the minds of its employees in addition to the monetary capital invested in hardware, plant, machinery, and raw materials. Some researchers began to think about how important it might be for a company to *engage* its employees rather than to control them. Sometimes called the **Human Relations Movement**, the new approach was characterized by companies beginning to pay more attention to individuals and their motivational needs, reflecting a growing belief that if the employees prospered, the company would also benefit.

The Human Relations Movement really had its roots in Elton Mayo's famous **Hawthorne Works experiments** during the 1920s. (The experiments took place at the Hawthorne, Illinois, plant of the Western Electric Company.) During those experiments, Mayo studied the effects of various sorts of lighting on worker productivity. The results indicated that there were *no* discernable effects that one could ascribe to lighting, so Mayo began looking at other variables, including meals, rest breaks, the number of hours worked, etc. Unexpectedly, productivity went up at *every* change, and when everyone was returned to their original hours and conditions, productivity went up again. This seemed to indicate that the **social dynamic** (i.e., that the workers had begun to think of themselves as a team) had more to do with increasing productivity than did finding what Taylor would have called the "one best way" to accomplish their tasks.

Douglas McGregor, of the MIT Sloan School of Management, described **Theory Y,** an optimistic approach that was opposed to the more pessimistic **Theory X** that he felt was often employed. While Theory X stressed strict supervision, direct managerial control, and external motivators, Theory Y was more optimistic: it presumed that providing job satisfaction, self-determination, and autonomy actually yielded better results.

Contemporary Management Theories

In the mid-60s and beyond, Blake & Mouton employed a **management grid** to describe management styles by placing those styles on a matrix that plotted "concern for people" along one axis, and "concern for production (or tasks)" along the other. Leaders were placed in one or more quadrants, based on how they scored on a questionnaire. The idea was that there was a "sweet spot" on the grid; the most desirable place for a leader would be to score highly on both the Task and People measures, but with the understanding that certain situations may call for the other quadrants to be used. For instance, there are times when being authoritarian might serve a manager (and the team) well by instilling a sense of discipline.

In the 1990s, Peter Senge wrote (in *The Fifth Discipline: The Art and Practice of the Learning Organization*) that managers need to think of businesses as complex, growing systems—i.e., as organic entities that constantly respond to various feedback mechanisms. Gone were the days of the staid, stable company that could operate in the same way 20 years after its founding as it did when first established.

Also in the 1990s, **business process management (BPM)** emerged as a tool to help improve company efficiency and responsiveness. BPM focuses on improving a company's business processes, in some ways recalling Taylor's mechanistic views of "the one best way" to accomplish and optimize tasks. But central to the modern interpretation is the idea that managers should concentrate on *processes* used to complete tasks, rather than just on the tasks themselves. In fact, one key to the success of BPM is that it forces businesses (i.e., managers) to realize that processes are in fact necessary in the first place, and that these processes should be thoughtfully, purposely, and purposefully designed, rather than simply having evolved.

Daniel Pink, in his 2011 book, *Drive*, examined motivation and argued that the old reward/punishment paradigm was no longer an effective approach to employee motivation. Instead, he proposed that three things motivate people: **autonomy** (control over one's life), **mastery** (the need to achieve and to improve), and **purpose** (the desire to be a part of something larger than ourselves, and to act in service of that larger something).

Management approaches continue to evolve, with companies facing new challenges in data management and security, and also attempting to address new technologies and legal requirements. As a result, companies continue to seek new management techniques and tools to help them deal with this dynamic new environment.

Knowledge and Skill Requirements

The global and technical nature of modern organizations calls for managers who possess the following range of skills:

- Technical
- Analytical
- Decision-making
- Conceptual
- Computer
- Communication
- Interpersonal

Technical skills refer to the ability to perform a specific task that requires knowledge of certain techniques, processes, and resources. Engineering directors, sales managers, and construction supervisors must have technical skills in their field to manage workers and to solve problems. For example, a director of an accounting department needs to understand accounting practices, while a nursing director needs the skills to perform medical procedures. Frontline managers require more technical skills than middle- and top-level managers do because frontline managers deal with daily operations and problems.

Analytical skills refer to a manager's ability to identify problems and develop solutions. Reasoning capabilities are necessary to understand a complex issue, but computer software is available to assist in analyzing data. Supervisors use software to monitor inventory, oversee budgets, and manage staff assignments. Such analytical tools assist managers in diagnosing, evaluating, and solving problems in the workplace.

Managers at every level of an organization use **decision-making skills** on a daily basis. Effective managers separate themselves from ineffective managers by the quality of their decisions. Analytical skills influence decision-making skills, and inadequate reasoning leads to poor decisions. In some instances, supervisors seek advice from a group before making a choice that involves several options, but some problems require quick decisions.

In conjunction with analyzing situations and making decisions is the capacity to understand the big picture. **Conceptual skills** refer to a supervisor's ability to perceive the objectives and strategies of an organization, to realize the interconnections within an organization, and to comprehend the role of the firm in the outside world. Top-level managers utilize their conceptual skills frequently as they make decisions regarding a firm's long-term strategy. For example, the CEO of a corporation attempts to forecast the future when considering mergers, acquisitions, and investments.

Computer skills are necessary for the success of today's managers. Managers do not necessarily need to know how to write programs, but they do need to know how to use business software. Supervisors must be proficient with software in order to generate spreadsheets, create presentations, schedule meetings, and manipulate data. Web-based businesses require supervisors who have the computer skills to monitor digital sales, manage international supply chains, and oversee website development. Quickly changing technology calls for supervisors who have both the technical knowledge and the desire to advance their computer skills.

Communication and interpersonal skills are closely connected concepts in management. The ability to convey ideas clearly is essential for success because managers communicate with employees and executives constantly. **Communication skills** refer to the ability to explain ideas orally or in writing to others. Effective managers encourage questions from employees to make certain everyone is on the same page. Managers who need results from their employees must clearly communicate what is required or everyone fails. Supervisors need **interpersonal skills**, or **people skills**, to develop strong relationships with other members of the organization. Managers spend the bulk of their days interacting with people, so the ability to lead, motivate, understand, and work with others is critical to success. Often supervisors fail due to a lack of people skills rather than a lack of technical or analytical skills. Showing appreciation, listening actively, resolving conflicts, expressing empathy, and creating a positive work environment are skills not often taught in school, but they are the characteristics of excellent supervisors.

Managers at every level actively work to acquire and develop the skills needed for efficient supervision in the workplace. Frontline, middle-level, and top-level managers need computer skills, interpersonal skills, decision-making skills, and communication skills. Frontline managers use technical skills often because they are close to employees who are performing specific technical tasks. Middle management and top management positions call for analytical skills, while top executives in an organization require conceptual skills.

Managerial Roles

A **role** is a job-related behavioral expectation. **Henry Mintzberg**, a Canadian academic, has conducted research and written books about management. Mintzberg's most often cited study involved observing and interviewing five CEOs from different industries over a two-week period. Upon reviewing the information he collected, Mintzberg identified the following ten roles of managers:

1. Figurehead
2. Leader
3. Liaison
4. Monitor
5. Disseminator
6. Spokesperson
7. Entrepreneur
8. Disturbance Handler
9. Resource Allocator
10. Negotiator

Since many of the roles are closely related, Mintzberg sorted them into three general categories:

1. Interpersonal
2. Informational
3. Decisional

The interpersonal roles—figurehead, leader, and liaison—stem from the formal authority of a supervisor and the interpersonal skills used in the position. Most managers are required to serve as figureheads when they perform ceremonial duties or receive visitors. Examples include a high school principal handing out diplomas to graduates and a manufacturing manager giving a tour of a new facility to stockholders. In the leadership role, a manager directs and coordinates the duties of subordinates. As a leader, a manager hires and fires personnel and ensures that tasks are progressing properly. The liaison role requires managers to maintain communication with individuals inside and outside of an organization. In general, the interpersonal roles of a manager relate to providing information to others and developing interpersonal relationships.

As a monitor, disseminator, and spokesperson, a manager processes information. In the **informational role**, a manager receives and sends information. As a monitor, a manager assesses the successes, problems, and opportunities that may affect a unit, such as trends or sales. Managers act as disseminators by relaying confidential information to subordinates, such as when a CEO learns about quality concerns from a large customer and instructs a vice president to handle the problem personally. The role of disseminator often requires a manager to filter information and to delegate responsibilities. A manager represents a unit or a group of people when acting as a spokesperson internally or externally. For example, a sales manager may attempt to persuade executives to pay bonuses to the sales team when acting as an internal spokesperson. When serving as an external spokesperson, a manager serves in a public relations capacity by representing the views of the organization to outsiders, such as civic organizations or the media.

Entrepreneur, disturbance handler, resource allocator, and negotiator are elements of the **decisional role**. Many people consider the decisional role more important than a manager's interpersonal or informational roles. Making improvements to the unit is the objective of the entrepreneurial role. For example, a restaurant manager is constantly planning changes to the menu and the service to meet customer needs. Taking quick measures to control immediate problems and to create stability is an aspect of the disturbance handler role. A frontline manager who responds to broken equipment or striking workers is acting as a disturbance handler attempting to return the work environment to normal. The resource allocator determines how to distribute limited resources, such as money, people, time, and equipment. Decisions regarding how many workers to assign to a project and how much money to allocate for upgrading office equipment are related to a manager's role as resource allocator. As negotiators, managers bargain with others to acquire benefits for their unit. Executives negotiate salaries and benefits with labor union representatives, and office managers negotiate work schedules with employees.

The ten roles of a manager illustrate the following three general ideas:

1. The roles explain what management entails and illustrate how the roles are connected.
2. Neglecting one or more of the roles prevents subordinates from working effectively.
3. The significance of each role illustrates the need for supervisors to manage their time well.

According to Mintzberg, managers need to be both specialists and generalists for success in any organization. A specialist is an expert at a specific discipline, such as marketing, accounting, or sales. A generalist has a broad understanding of a variety of business elements that provides managerial perspective. The numerous roles expected of managers call for varied skills to handle complex situations.

Levels of Management

Most large organizations have three different levels of management: frontline (also referred to as first-level or first-line), middle-level, and top-level. A **frontline manager** is a lower-level manager within an organization. Depending on the organization, a frontline manager may be referred to as a supervisor, office manager, foreman, or operational manager. Whatever the title, a frontline manager oversees daily operational activities and serves as the connection between management and employees. Frontline managers supervise the work of various units within an organization, such as sales, marketing, accounting, production, and information technology.

Middle-level managers oversee frontline managers and report to top-level managers. Tactical manager, department manager, plant manager, and director of operations are other titles for middle-level managers. Middle-level managers translate the ideas and objectives developed by top-level executives into specific goals and activities for frontline managers. A middle-level manager interprets corporate objectives into plans for the different units within an organization. Beginning in the early 1990s, corporate reorganizations no longer affected only blue-collar workers. In addition, reorganizations began eliminating many middle-level management positions, a trend that has continued though the financial crisis of the early 2000s and into the current business climate. Flatter, leaner organizations are more desirable; these theoretically have the flexibility to adapt quickly.

Top-level managers, or strategic managers, are the smallest and highest tier of management. The senior executives in an organization, such as the chief executive officer, chief operating officer, president, and vice president, constitute top-level management. Responsible for the performance and effectiveness of an organization, a top-level manager reports to the board of directors, owners, and stockholders of a corporation. Top-level managers concentrate on the long-term issues and growth strategies that middle-level managers broadcast to frontline managers for implementation.

Business Ethics

Ethics are a system of rules that distinguishes between right and wrong. **Business ethics** refer to the moral principles that dictate behavior in the business realm. In most cases, customers, society, competitors, and special interest groups judge whether a business acts ethically. However, attempts have been made to institute **universal business ethics**, with the most successful being the **CRT Principles of Business**, also known as the **Caux Principles**. In 1986, an international network of principled business leaders founded the Caux Round Table for Moral Capitalism (CRT). Along with business leaders from Europe, Japan, and the US, this group drafted the CRT Principles for Business, a comprehensive set of ethical guidelines aimed at helping international and multicultural businesses. Formally launched in 1994, the principles place an emphasis on showing concern for human dignity and working for the common good, a concept known as **kyosei**. The CRT Principles of Business have been published in 12 different languages and are considered the most comprehensive set of responsible business practices formed by business leaders for business leaders.

Although universal ethical principles are useful, laws are often required to ensure ethical business practices. In response to corporate scandals, such as those at Enron and WorldCom, the US Congress enacted the **Sarbanes-Oxley Act** in 2002. The law sets strict accounting and reporting rules that make top-level managers more accountable in an attempt to promote ethical behavior within public companies. In addition to laws, business ethics are influenced by ethical standards established within organizations. A company's code of ethics typically addresses conduct of employees, shareholders, customers, and suppliers.

Some organizations develop corporate ethics programs. In addition to an ethics code, an ethics program establishes committees to investigate ethics violations, communication systems to help employees report violations, and disciplinary procedures for employees found guilty of unethical activities. Ethics programs are either compliance-based, integrity-based, or somewhere in between.

- **Compliance-based ethics programs** are designed by an organization's lawyers to prevent, expose, and discipline violations; these programs involve establishing legal procedures and having top-level managers monitor compliance.
- **Integrity-based ethics programs** are designed to instill personal and ethical responsibility among employees; organizations and workers self-govern based on established guidelines with which they concur.

Corporate Social Responsibility

Corporate social responsibility refers to the obligations that a business has toward society. A socially responsible company attempts to increase the positive impact it has on society and decrease its negative impact. Social responsibilities are divided into four major categories:

1. *Economic responsibility:* produce goods and services that society desires and that are profitable
2. *Legal responsibility:* obey local, state, federal, and international laws
3. *Ethical responsibility:* meet society's moral expectations
4. *Philanthropic responsibility:* participate in desirable behaviors and activities, such as contributing to charities

In recent years, many businesses have combined the concepts of social responsibility and capitalism: socio-capitalism. Once considered divergent philosophies, profit and social responsibility have been blended in many for-profit businesses, such as those that provide services to the poor or the physically impaired.

MANAGEMENT FUNCTIONS

In the early 1900s, **Henri Fayol,** a French business owner, developed the first general theory of management. Fayol wrote a book about his management experiences in the mining industry. He expressed the idea that professional management involves five primary functions: planning, organizing, leading, coordinating, and controlling. Despite the numerous books that have been written in the last century about management, **Fayolism** remains the most influential theory. However, Fayol's original five functions have been reduced to four, which are discussed in the next sections:

1. Plan
2. Organize
3. Lead
4. Control

TIP: Although planning is difficult due to the fluctuating nature of direct and indirect forces, effective and efficient managers develop plans to handle future changes in the business environment.

Planning

Planning is the first function of management and directs the way in which managers organize, lead, and control. Planning requires managers to create proactive plans to accomplish the goals and objectives of an organization. Managers consider a number of factors when developing plans:

- **Resources:** organizational, human, financial, and physical
- **Opportunities and risks:** innovations, competition, and demand

Planning is a process of making decisions. The following table outlines the six basic steps involved in the planning process.

Planning Process

Step 1: Situational analysis	• Process used by planners to gather, analyze, and summarize relevant data • Process reviews past events, identifies current conditions, anticipates future trends, and considers internal and external forces • Results in identification of decisions that need to be made and helps managers decide whether to move to next step in process
Step 2: Alternative goals and plans	• Generate alternate goals (desired targets) and plans (actions to achieve goals) • Stress creativity and open minds of managers and employees
Step 3: Goal and plan evaluation	• Evaluate pros, cons, and possible outcomes of each alternative goal and plan • Prioritize and eliminate goals and plans
Step 4: Goal and plan selection	• Select plan and goal that is most practical and possible • Requires experienced judgment
Step 5: Implementation	• Implement the chosen plan once managers and employees understand the plan and the necessary resources become available
Step 6: Monitor and control	• Monitor subordinates regarding implementation of the plan • Create control systems to measure performance and take corrective actions when necessary

It should be noted that in Step 2, there are three different types of plans that may be developed. **Single-use plans** are intended to accomplish a set of goals one time only. An example of a single-use plan is a grand opening celebration for the opening of a new hospital wing. **Standing plans** are established for ongoing activities that accomplish constant goals, such as a corporation's plan to recruit minorities. Standing plans often develop into corporate policies. **Contingency plans** are established when an initial plan fails or events call for immediate changes. Many organizations have contingency plans for dealing with major disasters to make sure that both data and employees stay safe.

Levels of Planning

Just as there are three levels of management—frontline, middle-level, and top-level—there are three levels of planning that vary in scope and activities.

1. *Strategic planning* focuses on an organization's long-term (more than five years) goals and strategies in general terms. Developed by top-level managers, strategic plans clarify the company's mission and goals for the future. For example, a firm's strategic plan may involve penetrating a new market.
2. *Tactical planning* involves developing specific and intermediate-term (two to five years) goals and plans for implementing elements of the strategic plan. For example, tactical plans, which are implemented by middle management, may include designing and testing equipment needed for a new product.
3. *Operational planning* involves translating tactical plans into specific steps in the short-term (less than two years). Frontline managers implement operational plans, which may require scheduling production runs and staffing.

Strategic Management

In the past, strategic plans filtered downward from the top of an organization, but, in recent years, tactical and operational managers have participated in the strategic planning process. Top executives have learned through experience that middle-level and frontline managers offer valuable input and ideas. **Strategic management** is the term used to describe the process of multi-level managers working together to develop and implement a firm's goals and strategies. The strategic management process is composed of six steps:

1. Establish mission, vision, and goals
2. Analyze external opportunities and threats
3. Analyze internal strengths and weaknesses
4. Perform a SWOT analysis and formulate strategy
5. Implement strategy
6. Implement strategic control system

In the first step of the strategic management process, managers develop a mission statement that conveys the purpose of the organization. Effective mission statements focus on the customer, and they are attainable, inspirational, and specific. A strategic vision is the desired future direction of an organization, while strategic goals are the primary targets.

The mission, vision, and goals of an organization drive the second step of the process, which is analyzing the external environment. Managers study industry growth rates, market segments, and consumer purchasing power. Managers also analyze competitors, political activity related to the industry, social issues, labor issues, macroeconomic conditions, and technological factors.

During the third step, managers conduct an analysis of the strengths and weaknesses of significant internal components, such as finances, human resources, marketing activities, and manufacturing capabilities. Management also assesses the resources of the organization to determine its core competencies. **Core competencies** refer to the special skills or knowledge held by organizations that are especially valuable and rare. The core competence of a company is what it does better than the competition. For example, the core competence of Intel is complex chip design, while the core competence of Honda is small engine manufacturing.

After managers have gathered the information regarding the external and internal environment, they perform a SWOT analysis. A **SWOT analysis** is a comparison of the organization's strengths, weaknesses, opportunities, and threats, and it provides managers with a helpful way to summarize the relevant information gathered in the environmental analysis. Managers then formulate three levels of strategy based on the SWOT analysis.

Levels of Strategy

Corporate-level strategy	• Focuses on the big picture and how to accomplish the organization's goal • May involve concentration on a single business, diversification, or vertical integration
Business-level strategy	• Focuses on the way in which a business competes in a specific industry or market for competitive advantage • May implement a low-cost strategy to make basic, inexpensive products or a differentiation strategy to make unique, high-quality products
Functional-level strategy	• Implemented by functional units in an organization, such as production, human resources, marketing, finance, and distribution • Creates value for the consumer

In the fifth step of strategic planning, managers monitor whether strategies are being implemented appropriately. **Strategy implementation** requires middle-level and frontline managers to define strategic tasks, evaluate the organization's ability to complete the tasks, create an agenda for implementation, and develop an implementation plan. Implementation is followed by **strategic control**, which is a system that helps managers evaluate the organization's progress and correct problems when necessary.

Organizing and Staffing

Structuring a company's human and physical resources in a way that achieves organizational objectives is the process of **organizing**. Tasks, people, and departments all require organization to accomplish a company's goals. One of the initial steps in organizing is determining the organizational structure, which is the configuration of tasks and departments in a business. Organization charts visually clarify the reporting structure and levels of management. Differentiation and integration form the basis of organizational structure.

- **Differentiation:** an organization consists of different units that work on different tasks with different work methods and skills. Differentiation occurs through the division of labor and task specialization.
- **Integration:** the extent that different units in an organization coordinate their efforts to create a product or service.

Organizations with numerous specialized tasks and units are highly differentiated. In such businesses, there is a greater need for integration to ensure that all areas of an organization are working toward accomplishing the same goal.

Authority in Organizations

Authority in an organization refers to the sanctioned right to make a decision or tell others what to do. For example, the vice president of sales has the authority to give an order to a sales representative. Hierarchy establishes authority in an organization. In private businesses, the owners hold the greatest authority, but in publicly owned businesses, stockholders are the owners. Since stockholders lack the most current information needed to make wise decisions, a board of directors oversees an organization.

A board of directors serves four primary duties:

1. Choosing, evaluating, rewarding, and, when necessary, replacing the CEO
2. Assessing an organization's financial performance
3. Deciding an organization's strategic direction
4. Monitoring an organization's ethical, legal, and socially responsible activities

A board of directors is also responsible for reporting to stockholders, protecting the rights of stockholders, and advising management. As the senior member of top-level management, a CEO reports to the board of directors and is responsible for a firm's performance.

An important aspect of an organization's structure is its **span of control**, which is the number of subordinates who report to one manager. Wide spans form flat organizations with many workers reporting to one manager. A narrow span creates a tall organization with numerous reporting levels and fewer workers reporting to one manager. The ideal span of control depends on a number of variables:

- Competence of manager and workers
- Similarity or dissimilarity of tasks
- Amount of interaction required
- Degree to which tasks are standardized

Authority in an organization is dispersed over management levels and spans of control, so delegation is important. **Delegation** refers to assigning responsibilities to subordinates, and it occurs at every level of an organization as a method of accomplishing tasks through other people. Delegating authority forms a chain of command that defines the line of authority from the top of an organization to the bottom.

TIP: A chain of command specifies a reporting relationship for communicating both upward and downward in an organization.

Managers who delegate assignments must consider the ideas of responsibility, authority, and accountability. **Responsibility** refers to an employee's obligation to carry out an assigned task. Managers must ensure that a subordinate who has a specific responsibility has the necessary authority. Does the worker have the power to make decisions and give orders? Is the worker able to use necessary resources to fulfill the responsibility? In many cases, subordinates are given responsibilities for which they have no authority. The effective use of delegation saves managers time, and it raises the quality of subordinates.

The delegation of **authority** in an organization is either centralized or decentralized. In centralized businesses, high-level managers make major decisions. Authority is distributed throughout a decentralized organization. Decentralization benefits an organization by helping managers at all levels develop decision-making skills. Moreover, the managers who are the most knowledgeable about a problem are the most qualified to make a decision.

In conjunction with responsibility and the delegation of authority is the concept of accountability. **Accountability** refers to the expectation that a worker will perform a job and that failure to do so will result in corrective measures. One method of accountability involves requiring status reports from subordinates regarding assigned tasks.

Horizontal Structure

The concepts of authority, span of control, and decentralization relate to the vertical nature of an organization, but the horizontal structure is equally important. **Departmentalization** refers to the process of subdividing a business into smaller units or departments. One of the primary methods of subdividing work is by distinguishing line departments from staff departments. **Line departments** are responsible for the primary activities of the organization, which may be making things, selling things, or providing customer service. At Ford Motor Company, line departments include product design, assembly, and distribution. **Staff departments** support line departments with people who have specialized or professional skills. Types of line departments at Ford include accounting, legal, public relations, and human resources.

Organizations vary in the way they departmentalize, as indicated by the following table.

Ways to Departmentalize

Functional organization	• Units grouped according to specific activities like production, marketing, finance, and human resources • Common in large and small businesses but best in stable environments • Efficient use of resources • Discourages communication across departments
Product organization	• Units grouped around a specific product or product line • Clear task responsibilities • Flexibility makes it suitable for unstable environment • Costly duplication of effort
Customer organization	• Units grouped to serve customer needs, such as commercial or consumer accounts at a bank • Costly duplication of activities
Geographic organization	• Units grouped by defined territories, districts, regions, or countries • Useful for firms with varying customer needs and characteristics • Used most by multinational corporations • Requires large and costly staff at headquarters
Matrix organization	• Blending of functional and product organizations • Originated in aerospace industry • Dual line of command • Workers placed in teams for specific tasks • Decentralized decision-making • Vast communications network • Can cause confusion regarding authority

Staffing

Skilled individuals are the most important element of any organization, so staffing is a critical part of any manager's job. Recruitment, selection, and outplacement are the three primary staffing functions in organizations. **Recruitment** refers to attracting a pool of job candidates with the skills and attitudes beneficial to an organization. Advertising, visiting universities, and using private employment agencies are some of the ways in which businesses recruit employees.

During the selection process, an organization chooses the best candidate for a position. Selection tools may include applications, résumés, interviews, background checks, drug tests, and performance tests. Whatever the screening method, managers should be aware of legal and illegal activities during staff selection.

Legal and Illegal Screening Activities

Legal	Illegal
Asking if a person is authorized to work in the United States	Asking for proof of citizenship
Asking if a person has been convicted of a crime	Asking if a person has been arrested
Asking for proof of age after hiring	Requiring a birth certificate
Keeping records for recording purposes about racial and ethnic identity	Asking for race, creed, or national origin on application or during interview

Staffing decisions involve more than recruiting and screening. Difficult economic times often force companies to downsize by laying off many employees at once. At such times, many firms offer outplacement services. **Outplacement** refers to the process of assisting dismissed workers find new jobs.

Leading

Management positions in an organization offer the opportunity to exhibit leadership, which involves making changes and creating a vision for a firm. Successful leaders motivate others to overcome obstacles and accomplish organizational goals. At the core of effective leadership is **power**, the ability to influence other people to do something that they might not otherwise do. In a business setting, managers have five potential power sources.

Power Sources	
Reward power	Leader controls valued rewards, such as pay raises, promotions, and bonuses.
Coercive power	Leader controls punishments that people want to avoid, such as below-average performance evaluations.
Expert power	Leader has expertise or knowledge that people trust or believe.
Referent power	Leader has personal characteristics that trigger loyalty and admiration in others.
Legitimate power	Leader has the authority to tell others what to do, so people are obligated to comply.

Classic Approaches to Understanding Leadership

The three most widely accepted classic approaches for understanding leadership are the trait approach, the behavioral approach, and the situational approach.

Trait theory was the earliest attempt to define leadership qualities. In the early 20th century, researchers and scholars studied hundreds of leadership traits in an attempt to uncover the personal characteristics shared by exceptional leaders. The trait theory assumes that leaders are born with characteristics such as self-assurance, intelligence, sociability, and aggressiveness. However, upon completion of the study, scholars determined that no specific characteristics were essential for someone to become a great leader. The modern perspective regarding trait theory is that some personality attributes appear to separate successful leaders from other people. Drive, integrity, self-confidence, and business knowledge distinguish leaders from followers.

The **behavioral theory of leadership** attempts to identify the behaviors of effective leaders. Experts have identified three general leadership behavior categories: task-oriented, people-oriented, and directive/participative leadership.

Leader Behaviors

Category	Definition	Example Behaviors
Task-oriented	Task-oriented leaders focus their behaviors on the organizational structure and operating procedures and they tend to seek to control staff while focusing on the task at hand.	Initiating, setting goals, praising good work, supervising work quality.
People-oriented	People-oriented leaders attempt to ensure that the inner needs of people are satisfied, so they seek to motivate people by emphasizing the needs of staff members.	Showing concern for people's feelings, expressing appreciation, initiating, organizing, and clarifying.
Directive or Participative Leadership	**Directive (Autocratic):** This approach leaves all decisions in the hands of management and gives instructions with the full expectation of having them followed; sometimes referred to as the "my way or the highway" approach.	Not soliciting input from employees, making all company decisions, mandating methods, procedures and policies; exhibiting little or no trust in the decision-making, ideas, suggestions, or advice of employees
	Participative (Democratic): This approach involves all team members in identifying goals, developing strategies, and in arriving at ways to achieve those goals. Actions are taken to involve employees in decision-making.	Soliciting input from employees, encouraging employees to identify performance gaps, using employee satisfaction surveys, rewarding employees for innovative ideas, and allowing employees to identify their own strengths and weaknesses.

The **Leader-Member Exchange (LMX) theory** relates to group maintenance behaviors. According to the LMX theory, group maintenance behaviors such as trust, mutual respect, mutual loyalty, and open communication form the basis of satisfying personal relationships with group members.

Situational theorists assert that universal leadership traits and behaviors are nonexistent and that effective leadership varies from one situation to another. Effective leaders analyze a situation before making a decision. The **Vroom model** for decision-making and the **path-goal theory** are the primary situational models considered valid for modern management.

- **Vroom model:** a situational model proposed by Victor H. Vroom that helps leaders decide how much participation to use in decision-making. The model works like a funnel, asking the leader questions until reaching a recommended decision style. Decide, consult individually, consult the group, facilitate, and delegate are the five possible decision styles.
- **Path-goal theory:** a theory developed by Robert House that assesses characteristics of the followers and environmental factors before determining the appropriate leadership behavior. The four leadership behaviors are directive leadership, supportive leadership, participative leadership, and achievement-oriented leadership. Appropriate leader behaviors lead to effective performance from the followers.

Modern Theories on Leadership

While the historical views on leadership remain relevant today, contemporary experts have developed their own ideas about different leadership styles:

- **Charismatic leader:** Arouses excitement, holds strong moral convictions, and conveys extreme self-confidence
- **Transformational leader:** Motivates people to focus on good of the group rather than personal interests
- **Transactional leader:** Uses legitimate, reward, and coercive powers to give orders in exchange for benefits to followers
- **Level 5 leader:** Combines determination and humility to build long-term leadership
- **Authentic leader:** Uses honesty, genuineness, reliability, and integrity to lead others; willing to sacrifice own interests
- **Pseudo transformational leader:** Speaks about positive change for followers but power, control, wealth, and fame take priority

Motivation

An important aspect of leading is **motivation**, which refers to the set of forces that energize, guide, and maintain a person's efforts. Managers are responsible for motivating employees to be punctual, work well with others, and perform quality work. Setting goals for employees is a valuable motivational tool. For goals to be effective, they should be acceptable to workers, challenging, and achievable. Some of today's large organizations set stretch goals for employees. Stretch goals are especially difficult, but they are attainable. Firms have found that stretch goals push employees out of mediocrity and toward excellence.

Reinforcement is another method of encouraging or discouraging employee behavior. Organizational behavior modification attempts to change worker behavior and improve job performance by managing work conditions and applying consequences for specific actions.

- **Positive reinforcement:** give a consequence that will encourage the behavior to be repeated, such as a letter of commendation, pay raise, or positive performance evaluation
- **Negative reinforcement:** stop, remove, or avoid an unpleasant consequence, such as taking a worker off probation due to improved job performance
- **Punishment:** give an unpleasant consequence, such as criticizing an employee or assigning a worker to an undesirable task or shift
- **Extinction:** fail to give a reinforcing consequence by not complimenting an employee for doing a good job or setting unachievable performance goals

Positive reinforcement is utilized the most in business settings. Effective managers find creative ways to motivate employees by both monetary and nonmonetary means.

While reinforcement theory focuses on how the work environment motivates people's behavior, **expectancy theory** focuses on how people make behavioral decisions based on expected outcomes. Vroom's expectancy theory is one of the most widely accepted motivation theories, and it is based on three variables.

1. *Expectancy:* an employee's belief that increased efforts will lead to achieving performance goals
2. *Instrumentality:* an employee's belief that good job performance will lead to a specific outcome
3. *Valence:* the value that an employee places on a specific outcome

Expectancy theory proposes that employee motivation is a function of all three variables working together. The theory offers a general method of understanding the complex nature of employee motivation.

Content theories of motivation stem from the idea that people want to satisfy basic needs. The three main content theories are Maslow's hierarchy of needs, Alderfer's ERG theory, and McClelland's needs.

Content Theories of Motivation	
Maslow's hierarchy of needs	People satisfy needs in a specific order; the needs in ascending order are physiological, safety, social, esteem, and self-actualization
Alderfer's ERG theory	People have three basic sets of needs: existence, relatedness, and growth
McClelland's needs	People have three dominant needs: achievement, affiliation, and power

Controlling

Control is the fourth and final function of management. A control process directs employees toward achieving organizational goals and takes corrective measures when plans go unfulfilled. A lack of controls in an organization leads to any number of problems, such as poor product quality and employee theft. Three general methods exist for achieving organizational control.

1. *Bureaucratic control:* guides activities with formal rules, regulations, and authority, such as budgets and performance appraisals; best used for well-defined tasks and independent workers.
2. *Market control:* guides activities with pricing mechanisms and economic information, such as evaluation based on profits and losses; best used where output can be clearly identified.
3. *Clan control:* guides activities with norms, values, and trust with the assumption that the organization and the employee share the same interests; best used in environments where employees are empowered in decision-making and where there is no explicit way to complete a task.

The bureaucratic, or formal, control system is the one most commonly used in organizations, although market and clan controls are valid methods for regulating employee performance. However, for the purpose of this review, the focus will be on bureaucratic control systems.

Control systems usually consist of four steps:

1. Setting performance standards
2. Measuring performance
3. Comparing performance with the standard
4. Taking corrective action

A **standard** is a performance target for an organizational goal. Standards clarify the desired performance level, motivate employee performance, and act as benchmarks for performance assessment. Any activity or unit within an organization—financial, legal, ethical—can have a set of expected standards. Performance standards are based on quantity, quality, time used, and cost.

Measuring performance is the second stage of the control process. Managers measure employee or unit performance by counting the number of dollars earned, products sold, and items manufactured. Written reports, oral reports, and personal observations provide management with the data needed to measure performance.

The third step in the control process involves **comparing performance with the established standards**. This involves managers analyzing and evaluating performance results. According to the principle of exception, managers should focus attention on the cases that deviate significantly from the expected standard. For example, if five computer components out of every 1,000 produced on an assembly line are defective, a manager should investigate the five exceptions rather than the 995 other components. In addition, managers should not focus much time or effort on performance that is equal to or close to the standard. With the principle of exception, managers focus on the exceptions and not the norm to save valuable time.

The final step in the control process involves **taking corrective action** when significant deviations occur. During this step of control, adjustments are made to ensure that the planned results and goals are met. Corrective measures may be taken immediately by the manager or by subordinates involved directly with the problem. In the case of computerized manufacturing, two types of control may occur:

1. *Specialist control:* employees who operate computer-numerical-control (CNC) machines notify engineering specialists about equipment problems, and the specialist corrects the issue.
2. *Operator control:* trained operators repair problems as they occur, which can be more efficient than specialist control.

In addition to equipment malfunctions, corrective action may require altering a marketing approach, disciplining an employee, or providing specialized training for workers.

Managers choose from three approaches to bureaucratic control: **feedforward**, **concurrent**, and **feedback**.

1. *Feedforward control:* Focuses on preventing problems before they occur; enacted before operations start; involves policies, procedures, and rules that limit certain activities; also known as **preliminary control**
2. *Concurrent control:* Focuses on directing, monitoring, and modifying ongoing activities
3. *Feedback control:* Focuses on end results; uses performance data to correct deviations and guide future actions; Six Sigma is a feedback control tool used in manufacturing that aims to reduce defects

Auditing and Budgeting

A **management audit** is a type of control used to evaluate the effectiveness and efficiency of an organization. External audits are performed by an outside organization, such as an accounting firm. Internal audits are performed in-house to assess various elements of a firm, such as financial stability, public relations, social responsibility, and manufacturing efficiency.

Budgeting, or **budgetary controlling**, is a widely used control process that involves investigating what a firm has done. Results are compared with budget information for the purpose of verification and correction. Budgets connect feedforward, concurrent, and feedback controls. A budget guides the allocation of resources before an operation begins, which is a feedforward control. During the ongoing activities of an operation, budgets are monitored, which is a concurrent control. Feedback control occurs when sales and expenses are compared.

ORGANIZATIONAL ENVIRONMENT

The environment in which an organization functions influences many decisions, such as whether to expand, contract, build a new plant, or launch a new product. Many factors—both internal and external—make up the organizational environment.

Central to an organization's environment are **customers**, or **consumers**. Customers and consumers make or break a business, so they are the most critical direct environmental force. There are two types of consumers—final and intermediate. **Final consumers** purchase products in their completed form, such as a Wendy's hamburger or a pair of Nike running shoes.

An **intermediate consumer** buys raw materials or wholesale products and then sells the product to final consumers. For example, Macy's department store is an intermediate consumer that buys clothing from manufacturers and wholesalers. Similar to suppliers, consumers affect the price of products and services by demanding higher quality, better service, and lower prices. Savvy consumers know how to search for low prices, and the internet is a huge factor in enabling consumers to price shop, thereby forcing businesses to be more competitive.

Legal, Political, Economic, and Social Forces

Legal and political factors are two components of an organization's **macro environment**. Laws and political decisions play an important part in the success or failure of a business and are areas that management must pay attention to in order to respond quickly to changes. Laws, trade agreements, and rules are reflective of the political party in control as well as the social mores and values of the time and can help or hinder an organization. If an organization produces a product that society deems harmful, it can be subject to taxes and regulations that hinder success. For example, tobacco products, once considered harmless, are now subject to health warnings and increased taxes due to findings regarding tobacco's health hazards. On the other hand, if an organization produces goods or services more in line with the areas popular with legislators and voters, it may have a competitive edge. Similarly, the political decisions determine whether mergers are considered anticompetitive or harmless to the current business climate. Political decisions also determine whether the tax environment is friendly to organizations or whether it is more profitable to find an offshore location to expand business. Antitrust laws, trade regulations, and investment tax credits are legal forces that have an impact on businesses. While organizations can't control the laws passed, rules put in place, or tax codes, they must pay attention to these variables and be ready to shift focus when necessary in order to stay competitive.

In addition to the federal laws, local and state laws factor into this category of an organization's macro environment. Local and state governments have the power to write ordinances that provide advantages to organizations. They can offer tax incentives or make road improvements that are inviting for organizations looking for a place to set up headquarters or build a new plant. Alternatively, they can write ordinances that hinder building or create zoning that doesn't allow a particular type of manufacturing. Local and state government factors are yet another layer of the macro environment that managers must stay abreast of to remain competitive.

Regulators are an additional component of the legal factors involved in an organization's macro environment. Regulators are government agencies with the power to investigate and monitor businesses to ensure compliance with laws regarding workplace, product, and environmental safety. They are responsible for fining organizations guilty of illegal business practices. The Occupational Safety and Health Administration (OSHA), the Federal Aviation Administration (FAA), and the Environmental Protection Agency (EPA) are examples of regulatory agencies. In addition, the Securities and Exchange Commission (SEC) monitors US financial markets, and the Food and Drug Administration (FDA) oversees medical devices, pharmaceuticals, cosmetics, and food.

The **economy** is another environmental component that shapes management decisions and consumer demand. Economic factors include trade or import restrictions or arrangements in the country where an organization does business, any economic cycles such as recessions or downturns, monetary policies, and income distribution. Management considers all of these factors and expands production when the economy is strong and reduces production and cuts jobs during difficult economic times. Managers adjust staffing, operations, and prices based on inflation rates, interest rates, productivity, and unemployment rates. High interest and inflation rates affect the costs associated with borrowing money to expand a business and reduce consumer demand for products and services. Unemployment rates influence labor availability and wages. Energy sources and costs also have an impact on business by increasing or decreasing the expenses associated with running a business.

Another indirect environmental force on the economy is **technology**, which businesses use to meet consumer needs. Technological innovations in communication devices, television, software, medical devices, energy, robotics, and transportation change the way in which people live. Advancements in technology create new businesses and increase competition. Effective managers utilize technology to lower costs, increase production, and improve services and products.

Social forces also impact businesses. These can include workers' and customers' values, traditions, and behaviors; all are constantly changing, and businesses must change with them. Social media, for example, has changed how businesses operate. Younger consumers are especially inclined to shop more online; their lifestyles and buying habits may be different than those of the company's earlier customers. Companies must adapt in order to reflect—and take advantage of—these social changes.

Other social factors that can impact a business can include customers' education levels and disposable income, as well as family size and structure, life expectancy, and cultural diversity. In addition, changing attitudes toward career aspirations and leisure time can affect customers' behavior and expectations.

Labor-Management Relations

Each day, managers face the direct forces on an organization: competitors, suppliers, and customers. A **competitor** is any rival firm competing for the same group of customers. Colgate and Crest are rivals in the toothpaste market, while Mercedes and Lexus are rivals for luxury car buyers. Businesses attempt to distinguish themselves in the marketplace and stay ahead of rival firms. Because of this, managers must monitor the competition to determine if rivals are making significant product adjustments or launching sales promotions.

Suppliers provide businesses with capital, office supplies, information, parts, and raw materials, so they directly affect product quality. A motorcycle is composed of parts and materials from suppliers, so low-quality parts will result in a low-quality motorcycle. In addition to quality issues, the price of supplies affects the price of a product or service, which is why some businesses rely on multiple suppliers rather than only one. **Supply chain management** has become increasingly important to businesses wanting to stay competitive and profitable. Supply chain management refers to managing an extensive network of facilities and people involved in the process of acquiring raw materials, creating products, and distributing products to customers.

In some industries, such as auto, steel, and transportation, labor unions act as suppliers of workers. Although only about 10 percent of the US labor force belongs to a union, unions still wield significant power. Labor unions represent the interests of their members in issues related to hiring, salaries, working conditions, and job security. In the past, labor unions and managers were on opposite sides, but the relationship has improved over the years. Managers and labor unions realize the need to work collaboratively to increase productivity and to stay competitive in the marketplace.

Labor-management committees are one method of bringing labor and management together to negotiate contracts. Representatives from both sides meet to discuss solutions to problems, which often leads to mutual benefits and trust.

Unionized businesses often operate differently than nonunionized businesses. For instance, in most nonunionized companies, recruiting and staffing are handled by the company's human resources (HR) department. In a union environment, the union itself may recruit and staff positions within the company. Administration may also differ. In a unionized company, seniority is often the most important criterion when it comes to promotions or layoffs, and the demotion or laying off of employees may be subject to stipulations laid out in the contract between the company and the union.

Labor-management relations can also be affected by the classification of employees as either **exempt** or **nonexempt**. The former are generally salaried staff, and are "exempt" in the sense that they are excluded from overtime, minimum wage, and other regulations. Exempt staff are often considered "white collar" employees. Nonexempt employees are paid an hourly wage and are entitled to overtime pay under the Fair Labor Standards Act.

Organizational Culture

One particularly important aspect of an organization's internal environment is the company culture. **Culture** refers to the shared system of behavior, rituals, and practices of an organization's members. It should be inextricably linked to an organization's goals, strategies, and beliefs. The culture of one corporation differs from that of another, and it gives employees behavioral expectations to follow. For example, the culture at Walt Disney Company promotes dedication to customer satisfaction, while the culture at Southwest Airlines encourages customer fun.

Culture is built through the organizational socialization process, which occurs when managers and co-workers help newcomers develop the skills needed for acceptance into the corporate team. A strong organizational culture benefits a business by encouraging employee loyalty and cooperation.

Consider the field of advertising. The work requires long hours and a dedication to customers that asks a great deal of employees. Many agencies pay low entry-level salaries and still expect this level of effort. As a reward, they provide an atmosphere filled with perks and play that goes beyond the typical company picnic. Tech companies fall into this category as well. The rewards rise to such a level that employees are willing to work sixty hours a week, meet unrealistic deadlines, all with a positive attitude. By creating a culture that rewards this dedication, organizations keep employees happy enough to work at a breakneck pace and deliver for their clients.

However, sometimes corporate culture can become problematic. When it becomes unbending and stifling, it prevents change and growth. For many decades, IBM exerted a strong organizational culture, which later became counterproductive. The IBM culture resisted change and hindered the company's ability to compete against new computer firms like Apple and Compaq, which eventually grabbed a significant portion of IBM's market.

Global Forces and Workplace Diversity

Global forces, or the actions of countries around the world, are part of the indirect forces of an organization's macro environment. Managers face the challenge of competing with global firms in addition to local ones. As technology increases, it is becoming more common for businesses to compete on an international level. In the past, the size of an organization and its level of experience were the most important qualities to consumers. Today, speed and efficiency are qualities that count.

Foreign governments may subsidize certain industries or pass laws that protect certain types of businesses, creating a less than friendly business climate for organizations. International trade agreements, exchange rates, and multi-country economic associations, such as the Organization of Petroleum Exporting Countries (OPEC), also affect the viability of foreign markets.

Trade relationships are another piece of an organization's macro environment. Trade relationships—positive or negative—can impact organizations. For example, the decision to thaw relations between the United States and Cuba in 2016 has created economic opportunities for organizations in a variety of industries; those organizations are looking for ways to gain an advantage over their competitors.

Cultural considerations are an additional piece of the global factors of an organization's macro environment of the twenty-first century. For example, as large numbers of older, experienced people retire, managers must find new employees to replace them. Improved education and skill levels overseas have led many managers to outsource telemarketing and manufacturing jobs to India and other countries with low labor costs. This integration of different cultures requires managers to address the challenges arising from culturally based yet differing styles of leadership, motivation, and attitudes toward work. Additionally, an increasing number of immigrants and women in the workforce has created more **diversity** in businesses; their presence has helped to bring women's issues to the forefront of politics. Laws having to do with paid family leave are being discussed and considered by state and federal legislatures, with some states moving to passing family leave requirements. Managers are increasingly aware of the importance of providing equitable pay for men and women doing the same work, as well as equal opportunities for advancement up through the ranks of management. Health and social issues are also factors of concern. Many businesses are implementing programs that address mental stress, substance abuse, health care, career planning, and skills training.

Sustainable Environments

Businesses have always been expected to exhibit a certain level of social responsibility, but in recent decades that expectation has been expanded to include a responsibility to create a **sustainable** environment in more than one sense. Of course, companies must by definition be sustainable in order to last, and are thus able to continue creating jobs, in addition to the goods and services they sell.

In one sense, then, a sustainable business environment is one in which the business itself can thrive, because it is resilient, it creates economic value, and it contributes to strong communities. A business survives over the long term not simply because it delivers valuable products or services, but because it is part of a healthy system. Sustainability has become an increasingly important part of doing business.

That sustainability is also part of—and the result of—an organizational culture that encourages it. It is a culture in which employees share assumptions and beliefs about how the business should be run and about how it can contribute to social equity and a healthy environment.

The Environmental Component

More recently, the idea of a sustainable business has included doing as little harm to the environment as possible. Thus, the idea of sustainability has acquired an ecological component.

Many businesses now seek to operate in an environmentally responsible fashion, utilizing natural and green energy to the extent possible; the objective is for the businesses to act as a *steward* of natural resources, rather than merely as a consumer of them. One indicator of this new awareness is the popularity of **LEED certification**. LEED (Leadership in Energy and Environmental Design) is a program developed by the nonprofit US Green Building Council that rates the design, construction, and operation of buildings in terms of energy consumption and overall environmental safety. LEED-certified companies may qualify for tax breaks or other rewards, and may ultimately recoup extra costs simply because LEED-certified facilities are, in the long run, less expensive to operate.

Organizational Change

No organization can remain static and still thrive. It must respond to market forces, economic and cultural change, new technologies, and changes in the competitive arena. The secret to benefitting from organizational change is to *manage* those changes, rather than simply *respond* to them. In fact, an entirely new aspect of management, **organizational change management (OCM)**, has become prevalent as managers come to realize that change is inevitable, and that managed change can be beneficial (even profitable) while unmanaged or unplanned change is too often disruptive and confusing.

Not only is change guaranteed to occur, it appears to be occurring ever more rapidly, due to globalization (which provides more diverse markets for goods and services, but also more diverse sources of raw materials and labor), technological innovation, and other factors.

One of the most challenging tasks a supervisor will face occurs when a business undergoes organizational change. Reasons for organizational change can vary, from the relocation of office space within a building to the release of a new product, to the acquisition of another company. Because each of these changes can affect how employees do their jobs, it is imperative to the company's continued success that the employees continue to work as a team. Management will rely on the supervisors to lead the team while instilling confidence that the company will continue to maintain its identity and core values throughout whatever change occurs. By doing so, they can cultivate a culture of commitment and performance.

Human Factors

The key to successful organizational change is to acknowledge the **human factor**. When organizations change, people have to adjust. New leaders will be put in place, jobs and responsibilities will change, and new skills may be need to be developed. As a result, employees will be uncertain and may be resistant. To ensure success, a formal approach for managing change that involves all levels of the organization needs to be developed early and adapted often as change moves through the organization. Communication is vital. Management should take three important steps when organizational change is about to occur:

1. State the need or reason for the change.
2. Demonstrate its confidence in the company's future and leadership.
3. Provide a plan to direct decision-making and behavior.

Supervisors then must customize that information to apply to their workforce members, detailing the upcoming changes in terms of how it affects those individuals. In this way, a sense of ownership can develop throughout the organization early in the process of change.

Types of Change

There are four types of organizational change a business may undergo:

1. Organization-wide change vs. subsystem change
2. Transformational vs. incremental change
3. Remedial vs. developmental change
4. Unplanned vs. planned change

An **organization-wide change** involves the entire company. It could include such things as a major restructuring, significant layoffs, or equally significant staff additions. **Subsystem changes** might include department reorganization or the addition or removal of a product to or from a company's product line.

A **transformational** (or **quantum**) **change** is a radical one, often involving the reorganization of a company's entire management and reporting hierarchy. **Incremental changes**, in contrast, are small—sometimes continuous—improvements to processes or new computer systems brought online to work within the existing business framework.

Organizational change can be thought of in terms of the *goals* of the change. A **remedial change** is intended to remedy an issue, perhaps to rectify poor product performance or to encourage the company to become more proactive. **Developmental change**, on the other hand, may be aimed at making something that's already successful even *more* successful. For example, looking at ways to duplicate the success of one product by creating similar products.

Finally, **unplanned change** is usually in reaction to some unexpected, significant event—a sudden loss of a high-ranking executive, or a natural disaster that adversely affects production, or an inferior product performance that results in a rapid loss of customers—resulting in a rapid and usually disorganized response. These changes are often implemented on a short-term basis until a more permanent solution can be put in place. **Planned change** is the result of organizational leaders recognizing the need for major changes and being proactive and organized in their implementation. Planned changes are designed to be long-term solutions.

Workplace Safety and Security

A modern business cannot thrive without protecting its property and its people. In many cases, certain safety practices are *mandated* by government agencies, such as the **Occupational Safety and Health Administration (OSHA)**, which enforces the **Occupational Safety and Health Act of 1970**. OSHA requires that businesses carry out certain safety, hazard prevention, and training activities, and it provides guidelines and checklists for doing so. Workplace safety can include everything from employee training to requiring the use of certain protective equipment, such as earplugs and protective eyewear.

Shared Responsibility

In a business, everyone shares responsibility for workplace safety. The employer is responsible for leading the program and for providing safe working conditions. Managers are charged with developing appropriate attitudes and procedures to ensure that operations are carried out with due regard for safety. The employees are expected to comply with all safety-related rules and regulations.

OSHA Requirements

OSHA requires businesses to provide safety information to employees (in the form of Safety Data Sheets, for instance) and to keep records of work-related injuries or illnesses. Under certain circumstances, businesses are also required to put in place certain processes designed to protect employees. These can include, for example, lockout/tag out procedures (meant to immobilize or shield equipment currently undergoing maintenance or repair) and requirements governing who is allowed into dangerous or confined spaces.

In general, employers must abide by provisions of the Act that are meant to protect the company's employees. Among other requirements, companies must do the following:

- Provide a workplace free from serious recognized hazards.
- Comply with standards, rules, and regulations issued under the Act.
- Ensure that workplace conditions conform to applicable OSHA standards.
- Provide safe and properly maintained tools and equipment.
- Use color coded posters, labels, or signs to warn employees of potential hazards.
- Provide safety training in a language and vocabulary workers can understand.
- Provide medical examinations and training when required by OSHA standards.
- Post, at a prominent location within the workplace, the OSHA poster (or the state plan equivalent) informing employees of their rights and responsibilities.

Keep in mind that the above is not a complete list of requirements. See **https://www.osha.gov/as/opa/worker/employer-responsibility.html** for a more thorough explanation of the Occupational Safety and Health Act requirements.

SUMMING IT UP

- Effective managers facilitate the activities within organizations through **planning, organizing, leading,** and **controlling.** Managers use the **principles of supervision** to guide the work of others and to help an organization accomplish its short-term needs and long-term goals.
- Most large organizations have **three different levels of management: frontline, middle-level,** and **top-level or (strategic) managers.**
- The global and technical nature of modern organizations requires that managers possess a wide range of skills: **technical, analytical, decision-making, conceptual, computer, communication,** and **interpersonal.**
- The **ten roles of managers** identified by Canadian academic **Henry Mintzberg** are **figurehead, leader, liaison, monitor, disseminator, spokesperson, entrepreneur, disturbance handler, resource allocator,** and **negotiator.**
- **Ethics** are a system of rules that distinguish between right and wrong. **Business ethics** refer to the moral principles that dictate behavior in the business realm. **Ethics programs** are **compliance-based, integrity-based,** or somewhere in between.
- **Corporate social responsibility** refers to a business's obligations to society. Social responsibilities are divided into four major categories: **economic, legal, ethical,** and **philanthropic.**
- **Internal** and **external environmental factors** affect how an organization functions.
    - The **internal environment** includes employees, office layout, management style, and bonus systems.
    - The **external,** or **macro, environment** comprises "outside" factors that have direct effects (suppliers, competitors, customers) and indirect effects (legal, political, economic, technological, social-cultural, global) on daily operations.
- In the early 1900s, **Henri Fayol,** a French business owner, developed the first general theory of management. Fayol's four functions are **plan, organize, lead,** and **control.**
- The **three levels of planning** are **strategic, tactical,** and **operational.**
- A **SWOT analysis** is a comparison of an organization's **strengths, weaknesses, opportunities,** and **threats;** it enables managers to formulate three levels of strategy: **corporate, business,** and **functional.**
- A **board of directors** serves four primary duties: **choosing, evaluating, rewarding,** and, when necessary, **replacing** the CEO; **assessing** an organization's financial performance; **deciding** an organization's strategic direction; and **monitoring** an organization's ethical, legal, and socially responsible activities.

- It is important to be aware of the difference between **legal screening activities** and **illegal screening activities** during a job interview.
- The three most widely accepted classic approaches for understanding leadership are the **trait approach**, the **behavioral approach**, and the **situational approach**.
- **Vroom's expectancy theory**, one of the most widely accepted motivation theories, is based on three variables: **expectancy, instrumentality**, and **valence**.
- Contemporary **theories of leadership styles** include **charismatic, transformational, transactional, level 5, authentic**, and **pseudo transformational**.
- The three main **content theories** are **Maslow's hierarchy of needs**, **Alderfer's ERG theory**, and **McClelland's needs**.
- The three general methods for achieving organizational control are **bureaucratic control, market control**, and **clan control**.
- A **management audit** is a type of control used to evaluate the effectiveness and efficiency of an organization; it involves external and internal audits. **Budgeting**, or **budgetary controlling**, is a widely used control process that involves investigating what a firm has done.

Chapter 4

Principles of Supervision Post-Test

POST-TEST ANSWER SHEET

1. Ⓐ Ⓑ Ⓒ Ⓓ	16. Ⓐ Ⓑ Ⓒ Ⓓ	31. Ⓐ Ⓑ Ⓒ Ⓓ
2. Ⓐ Ⓑ Ⓒ Ⓓ	17. Ⓐ Ⓑ Ⓒ Ⓓ	32. Ⓐ Ⓑ Ⓒ Ⓓ
3. Ⓐ Ⓑ Ⓒ Ⓓ	18. Ⓐ Ⓑ Ⓒ Ⓓ	33. Ⓐ Ⓑ Ⓒ Ⓓ
4. Ⓐ Ⓑ Ⓒ Ⓓ	19. Ⓐ Ⓑ Ⓒ Ⓓ	34. Ⓐ Ⓑ Ⓒ Ⓓ
5. Ⓐ Ⓑ Ⓒ Ⓓ	20. Ⓐ Ⓑ Ⓒ Ⓓ	35. Ⓐ Ⓑ Ⓒ Ⓓ
6. Ⓐ Ⓑ Ⓒ Ⓓ	21. Ⓐ Ⓑ Ⓒ Ⓓ	36. Ⓐ Ⓑ Ⓒ Ⓓ
7. Ⓐ Ⓑ Ⓒ Ⓓ	22. Ⓐ Ⓑ Ⓒ Ⓓ	37. Ⓐ Ⓑ Ⓒ Ⓓ
8. Ⓐ Ⓑ Ⓒ Ⓓ	23. Ⓐ Ⓑ Ⓒ Ⓓ	38. Ⓐ Ⓑ Ⓒ Ⓓ
9. Ⓐ Ⓑ Ⓒ Ⓓ	24. Ⓐ Ⓑ Ⓒ Ⓓ	39. Ⓐ Ⓑ Ⓒ Ⓓ
10. Ⓐ Ⓑ Ⓒ Ⓓ	25. Ⓐ Ⓑ Ⓒ Ⓓ	40. Ⓐ Ⓑ Ⓒ Ⓓ
11. Ⓐ Ⓑ Ⓒ Ⓓ	26. Ⓐ Ⓑ Ⓒ Ⓓ	41. Ⓐ Ⓑ Ⓒ Ⓓ
12. Ⓐ Ⓑ Ⓒ Ⓓ	27. Ⓐ Ⓑ Ⓒ Ⓓ	42. Ⓐ Ⓑ Ⓒ Ⓓ
13. Ⓐ Ⓑ Ⓒ Ⓓ	28. Ⓐ Ⓑ Ⓒ Ⓓ	43. Ⓐ Ⓑ Ⓒ Ⓓ
14. Ⓐ Ⓑ Ⓒ Ⓓ	29. Ⓐ Ⓑ Ⓒ Ⓓ	44. Ⓐ Ⓑ Ⓒ Ⓓ
15. Ⓐ Ⓑ Ⓒ Ⓓ	30. Ⓐ Ⓑ Ⓒ Ⓓ	45. Ⓐ Ⓑ Ⓒ Ⓓ

46. Ⓐ Ⓑ Ⓒ Ⓓ   51. Ⓐ Ⓑ Ⓒ Ⓓ   56. Ⓐ Ⓑ Ⓒ Ⓓ

47. Ⓐ Ⓑ Ⓒ Ⓓ   52. Ⓐ Ⓑ Ⓒ Ⓓ   57. Ⓐ Ⓑ Ⓒ Ⓓ

48. Ⓐ Ⓑ Ⓒ Ⓓ   53. Ⓐ Ⓑ Ⓒ Ⓓ   58. Ⓐ Ⓑ Ⓒ Ⓓ

49. Ⓐ Ⓑ Ⓒ Ⓓ   54. Ⓐ Ⓑ Ⓒ Ⓓ   59. Ⓐ Ⓑ Ⓒ Ⓓ

50. Ⓐ Ⓑ Ⓒ Ⓓ   55. Ⓐ Ⓑ Ⓒ Ⓓ   60. Ⓐ Ⓑ Ⓒ Ⓓ

PRINCIPLES OF SUPERVISION POST-TEST
72 minutes—60 questions

Directions: Carefully read each of the following 60 questions. Choose the best answer to each question and fill in the corresponding circle on the answer sheet. The Answer Key and Explanations can be found following this post-test.

---

1. A frontline manager is responsible for

   A. translating the ideas and objectives developed by top-level executives into specific goals and activities.
   B. overseeing daily operational activities and serving as the connection between management and employees.
   C. interpreting corporate objectives into plans for the different units within an organization.
   D. concentrating on the long-term issues and growth strategies that an organization faces.

2. Which of the following persons developed the first theory regarding management functions?

   A. Winslow Taylor
   B. Henri Fayol
   C. Max Weber
   D. Henry Mintzberg

3. The process of teaching new employees the appropriate roles and behaviors needed to become effective members of a business is

   A. organizational socialization.
   B. cultural diagnosis.
   C. interpersonal development.
   D. managerial training.

4. Which of the following is a factor of an organization's macro environment, in addition to legal, political, economic, technological, and sociocultural factors?

A. Ethical
B. Local government
C. Global
D. Regulatory

5. A primary skill necessary at every level of management is

A. training.
B. technical.
C. conceptual.
D. decision-making.

6. Which of the following is characteristic of feedforward control?

A. Implementing transfer pricing
B. Monitoring ongoing data flow
C. Establishing rules and procedures
D. Evaluating performance results

7. Which theory is based on the idea that great leaders are born with self-assurance, integrity, and assertiveness?

A. Content theory
B. Path-goal theory
C. Trait theory
D. Behavioral theory

8. Labor unions traditionally focus on issues related to

A. salaries.
B. competitors.
C. managerial levels.
D. regulatory agencies.

9. Which of the following questions may legally be asked of a job candidate?

A. "How old are you?"
B. "What is your nationality?"
C. "May I see your proof of citizenship?"
D. "Have you ever been convicted of a crime?"

10. The process of different levels of managers working together to develop and implement organizational goals and strategies is

    A. systematic management.
    B. tactical management.
    C. administrative management.
    D. strategic management.

11. Which of the following is a contemporary management theory that focuses on improving a company's processes used to complete tasks, rather than improving the tasks themselves?

    A. Theory X
    B. Scientific management
    C. Theory Y
    D. Business process management

12. Which of the following control systems is most commonly used by firms?

    A. Clan
    B. Market
    C. Bureaucratic
    D. Organizational

13. An employee's belief that increased efforts at work will lead to accomplishing performance goals is known as

    A. equity.
    B. expectancy.
    C. task identity.
    D. instrumentality.

14. Which of the following has the power to regulate X-ray machines and blood glucose meters?

    A. Occupational Safety and Health Administration
    B. Environmental Protection Agency
    C. Food and Drug Administration
    D. Centers for Disease Control and Prevention

15. An increase in the cost of petroleum would affect a manufacturing company that used petroleum-based raw materials by

A. increasing employment costs.
B. decreasing transportation costs.
C. increasing manufacturing costs.
D. decreasing manufacturing costs.

16. Which of the following is developed to create consistency in situations repeatedly faced by an organization?

A. Single-use plans
B. Objectives
C. Standing plans
D. Scenarios

17. A sales manager who tries to make improvements in the sales department is functioning as a(n)

A. entrepreneur.
B. negotiator.
C. monitor.
D. liaison.

18. According to David McClelland, all of the following are people's primary needs EXCEPT:

A. Achievement
B. Power
C. Affiliation
D. Growth

19. Indirect external forces that influence decisions of whether to borrow money to expand a business include

A. material costs.
B. labor costs.
C. interest and inflation rates.
D. the end-of-year bonus payouts.

20. An intermediate consumer most likely purchases items from

A. retailers.
B. big box stores.
C. e-businesses.
D. wholesalers.

21. Which of the following combines aspects of feedforward, concurrent, and feedback control?

    A. Auditing
    B. Marketing
    C. Budgeting
    D. Financing

22. The extent that different work units work together to coordinate efforts is known as

    A. integration.
    B. organization.
    C. configuration.
    D. differentiation.

23. According to expectancy theory, the importance that an employee places on a specific outcome is known as

    A. valence
    B. motivation.
    C. legitimacy.
    D. instrumentality.

24. Which of the following is the most likely managerial benefit of technological advancements implemented in a manufacturing facility?

    A. Improved labor relations
    B. Increased production
    C. Lower energy costs
    D. Diverse workforce

25. As women and immigrants have entered the workforce, businesses have been forced to provide all of the following EXCEPT:

    A. More equitable compensation packages for men and women
    B. Jobs with pay scales dependent on an employee's gender
    C. Working environments that are respectful of the diverse backgrounds of all employees
    D. Equitable opportunities for promotion for both men and women

26. Which of the following best describes operational planning?

    A. Short-term time frame and low level of details
    B. Short-term time frame and high level of details
    C. Long-term time frame and low level of details
    D. Medium-term time frame and medium level of details

27. The Caux Principles were primarily developed to address

    A. business ethics.
    B. global commerce.
    C. accounting standards.
    D. environmental awareness.

28. Which of the following is established and implemented to help employees behave in the best interests of a business?

    A. Customer organization
    B. Mission statement
    C. Control system
    D. Tactical plan

29. Group maintenance behaviors can lead to the development of personal relationships with group members according to the

    A. LMX theory.
    B. LPC theory.
    C. Vroom theory.
    D. Hersey-Blanchard theory.

30. One of the potential benefits of developing a strong organizational culture is

    A. customer satisfaction.
    B. economic stability.
    C. ethics enforcement.
    D. employee loyalty.

31. Which of the following is characterized by high-level managers making the majority of decisions?

    A. Centralized organization
    B. High-involvement organization
    C. Decentralized organization
    D. Learning organization

32. Compliance-based ethics programs are designed to

A. encourage ethical behavior through rewards.
B. create interest in social responsibility efforts.
C. impose punishments upon ethics violators.
D. comply with global business guidelines.

33. The first step in the strategic management process is

A. analyzing potential opportunities.
B. formulating a functional strategy.
C. assessing strengths and weaknesses.
D. establishing a mission statement.

34. Stretch goals are best described as

A. straightforward.
B. prolonged.
C. impossible.
D. demanding.

35. What type of organizational change is primarily aimed at making something that's already successful even more successful?

A. Unplanned change
B. Developmental change
C. Remedial change
D. Transformational change

36. The concept that a business should seek to act as a steward of natural resources, rather than merely consuming these resources is one of the main objectives of

A. environmental scanning.
B. social responsibility.
C. internal strategies.
D. sustainability.

37. In an automobile manufacturing corporation, the accounting department is known as a

A. line department.
B. regional department.
C. staff department.
D. product department.

38. A company's culture can become problematic when it

    A. creates a sense of belonging that causes employees to display loyalty to the organization.

    B. is so well known that it creates an influx of applications for employment.

    C. stifles new ideas, the ability to change, and growth.

    D. enables staff to respond quickly to changes in the market.

39. Management reductions in recent years have mostly affected

    A. supervisors.

    B. middle management.

    C. chief executive officers.

    D. top management.

40. Which type of consequence is exemplified when a manager fails to show appreciation to an especially helpful subordinate?

    A. Positive reinforcement

    B. Punishment

    C. Negative reinforcement

    D. Extinction

41. Overseeing the interconnected network of facilities and people that take a product from the raw material stage to distribution is known as

    A. supply chain management.

    B. flexible manufacturing.

    C. egocentric management.

    D. strategic planning.

42. Which of the following is the result of a wide span of control?

    A. Few workers reporting to one supervisor

    B. Few workers reporting to multiple supervisors

    C. Many workers reporting to one supervisor

    D. Many workers reporting to multiple supervisors

43. All of the following are types of corporate-level strategies EXCEPT:

A. Vertical integration
B. Implementation
C. Diversification
D. Concentration

44. Task-specific knowledge refers to

A. communication skills.
B. analytical skills.
C. computer skills.
D. technical skills.

45. What is the most critical direct environmental force an organization faces?

A. Regulatory agencies
B. Technological innovations
C. Competitors
D. Customers

46. Which of the following methods of departmentalization is most commonly used by multinational corporations?

A. Product
B. Geographic
C. Matrix
D. Functional

47. Management decisions to outsource manufacturing jobs to foreign countries have primarily been influenced by

A. trade agreements.
B. immigration.
C. labor costs.
D. tax laws.

48. Which of the following developed a situational model of leadership that leads to five possible decision styles?

A. Henri Fayol
B. Fred Fiedler
C. Abraham Maslow
D. Victor Vroom

49. Which of the following has most likely used a differentiation strategy in pursuit of competitive advantage?

    A. Walmart
    B. Toshiba
    C. Porsche
    D. Hoover

50. A manager's ability to understand the strategies and objectives of a business is an aspect of

    A. decision-making skills.
    B. conceptual skills.
    C. interpersonal skills.
    D. analytical skills.

51. Managers who concentrate on significant deviations from anticipated standards are most likely using the principle of

    A. control.
    B. accountability.
    C. standardization.
    D. exception.

52. Government agencies that have the power to investigate business practices are known as

    A. prospectors.
    B. supervisors.
    C. regulators.
    D. defenders.

53. All of the following are primary duties of an organization's board of directors EXCEPT:

    A. Selecting the chief executive officer
    B. Making daily operational decisions
    C. Monitoring financial performance
    D. Determining strategic direction

54. Management activities such as hiring, training, and motivating workers are part of the

    A. figurehead role.
    B. leadership role.
    C. monitor role.
    D. resource allocator role.

55. Which of the following summarizes information gathered in an environmental analysis during the strategic planning process?

    A. ABC
    B. CRM
    C. LCA
    D. SWOT

56. All of the following are societal factors that indirectly influence businesses EXCEPT:

    A. Birth rate
    B. Productivity
    C. Immigration
    D. Life expectancy

57. A sales manager who reaches a deal with the CEO about implementing flexible scheduling for the sales unit is acting as a

    A. negotiator.
    B. liaison.
    C. figurehead.
    D. disseminator.

58. Exchange rates and trade agreements are examples of

    A. cooperative strategies.
    B. direct forces.
    C. entry barriers.
    D. indirect forces.

59. Studying the ten roles of a manager is important to realizing that

    A. all the roles are interconnected.
    B. technical and general skills are both essential.
    C. some roles are significantly more important.
    D. levels of management are complex.

60. Which of the following is a situational factor in the path-goal theory?

    A. Motivational methods
    B. Characteristics of leaders
    C. Leadership style
    D. Characteristics of followers

ANSWER KEY AND EXPLANATIONS

1. B	13. B	25. B	37. C	49. C
2. B	14. C	26. B	38. C	50. B
3. A	15. C	27. A	39. B	51. D
4. C	16. C	28. C	40. D	52. C
5. D	17. A	29. A	41. A	53. B
6. C	18. D	30. D	42. C	54. B
7. C	19. C	31. A	43. B	55. D
8. A	20. D	32. C	44. D	56. B
9. D	21. C	33. D	45. D	57. A
10. D	22. A	34. D	46. B	58. D
11. D	23. A	35. B	47. C	59. A
12. C	24. B	36. D	48. D	60. D

1. **The correct answer is B.** A frontline manager is responsible for overseeing daily operational activities and serving as the connection between management and employees. Choices A and C are responsibilities of the middle-level manager. Choice D describes the responsibilities of the top-level manager.

2. **The correct answer is B.** Henri Fayol developed the first theory of professional management functions, which include planning, organizing, leading, and controlling. Taylor (choice A) is regarded for improving industrial efficiency. Weber (choice C) was one of the leading founders of sociology. Mintzberg (choice D) identified the ten roles of managers.

3. **The correct answer is A.** Organizational socialization is the process of teaching new employees the appropriate roles and behaviors needed to become effective members of a business. Managers and co-workers help new workers develop the skills necessary for acceptance into an organization.

4. **The correct answer is C.** Global factors are a part of an organizations macro environment, in addition to legal, political, economic, technological, and sociocultural factors. Ethical (choice A) responsibility is a corporate social responsibility. The local government (choice B) and regulatory (choice D) are both categories within the legal component of the macro environment.

5. **The correct answer is D.** Decision-making skills are necessary at every level of management. Training workers and having technical skills (choices A and B) are most important for frontline managers who deal with blue-collar workers. Top-level managers must have conceptual skills (choice C) for making long-range goals.

6. **The correct answer is C.** Establishing rules and procedures before an activity begins is characteristic of feedforward control. Implementing transfer pricing (choice A) is not a characteristic of feedback control. Monitoring ongoing data (choice B) is an aspect of concurrent control. Feedback control involves evaluating performance results (choice D).

7. **The correct answer is C.** Trait theory is based on the idea that great leaders are born with characteristics such as self-assurance, integrity, and assertiveness. Content theory (choice A) is a motivational theory. Path-goal theory (choice B) and behavioral theory (choice D) are leadership theories that do not assert that people are born with leadership qualities.

8. **The correct answer is A.** Salaries, working conditions, hiring practices, and job security are the focus of most labor unions. Labor unions remain a significant direct force in industries such as auto and steel, although only about 10 percent of US workers are members. Competitors (choice B), managerial levels (choice C), and regulatory agencies (choice D) are less important issues to labor unions.

9. **The correct answer is D.** It is legal to ask a job candidate if he or she has been convicted of a crime; however, it is illegal to ask about arrests. Asking a person's age (choice A) can be done only after hiring. It is illegal to ask about a person's nationality (choice B) and for proof of citizenship (choice C).

10. **The correct answer is D.** *Strategic management* is the term for the process that brings together different levels of managers to develop and implement organizational goals and strategies. Systematic management (choice A) and administrative management (choice C) were two classical approaches toward management that did not involve different managerial levels. Middle-level managers are sometimes referred to as tactical managers (choice B).

11. **The correct answer is D.** Business process management (BPM) emerged in the 90s as a tool to help improve company efficiency and responsiveness. The focus is on improving processes used to complete tasks. Theory X (choice A) and Theory Y (choice C) are theories that emerged with the human relations movement. Theory X was a more pessimistic approach that stressed strict supervision, direct managerial control, and external motivators. In contract, Theory Y was more optimistic, focusing on providing job satisfaction, self-determination, and autonomy. Scientific management (choice B) was a theory promoted by Frederick Taylor where it was thought that businesses should be run in a scientific, efficient manner.

12. **The correct answer is C.** Bureaucratic control, which is also known as formal control, is the most commonly used control system within organizations. Clan control (choice A) is appropriate in flexible settings that allow employees to make decisions. Market control systems (choice B) are appropriate in situations where output can be clearly identified. Organizational (choice D) is not a control system.

13. **The correct answer is B.** According to the expectancy theory, expectancy is a person's belief that increased efforts at work will lead to accomplishing performance goals. Instrumentality (choice D) is the employee's belief that good job performance will lead to certain outcomes. Choices A and C are not variables in expectancy theory.

14. **The correct answer is C.** The Food and Drug Administration (FDA) monitors medical devices, such as X-ray machines and blood glucose meters, to ensure compliance with safety standards. OSHA and the EPA (choices A and B) are both regulatory agencies, but neither oversees medical devices. The CDC (choice D) is an agency of the US Department of Health and Human Services that provides information related to disease prevention and health improvement.

15. **The correct answer is C.** An increase in raw material costs impacts a business by increasing the costs of manufacturing, making choice D incorrect. Choice A is incorrect because unemployment rates, not raw material costs, influence labor rates. Choice B is incorrect because an increase in petroleum costs would likely increase transportation costs.

16. **The correct answer is C.** Standing plans are established for dealing with ongoing activities so that decisions can be made quickly, easily, and consistently. Standing plans often develop into company policies. Single-use plans (choice A) are developed for one-time situations. Objectives (choice B) and scenarios (choice D) are used in the planning process but are not developed for the sake of consistency.

17. **The correct answer is A.** According to Mintzberg, the entrepreneurial role of a manager involves making improvements to a unit. The negotiator (choice B) bargains with others to gain benefits, and the monitor (choice C) observes successes, failures, and problems that may affect the unit. As a liaison (choice D), a manager communicates with people inside and outside the organization.

18. **The correct answer is D.** According to McClelland, people's three main needs are achievement, affiliation, and power. Growth, existence, and relatedness are people's needs according to Alderfer's theory.

19. **The correct answer is C.** Interest and inflation rates are indirect external forces acting on an organization. Material costs (choice A), labor costs (choice B), and bonus pay outs (choice D) are all direct forces that act on an organization.

20. **The correct answer is D.** An intermediate consumer purchases items from wholesalers and manufacturers to make a finished product that will be sold to final consumers. Choices A, B, and C are incorrect because final consumers purchase goods from retailers, which include big box stores like Walmart and e-businesses.

21. **The correct answer is C.** Budgeting combines aspects of feedforward, concurrent, and feedback control. Budgets are established before a project begins, and they are monitored during a project. At the end of a project or activity, sales and expenses are compared for feedback.

22. **The correct answer is A.** Integration refers to the extent to which different units in an organization coordinate their efforts to create a product or service. Organizations that are highly differentiated need integration to make sure that all units work together to meet goals.

23. **The correct answer is A.** According to expectancy theory, valence refers to the importance that an employee places on a specific outcome. Vroom's expectancy theory analyzes what motivates people, so choice B is incorrect. Legitimacy (choice C) is not a part of the expectancy theory. Instrumentality (choice D) is a variable in the theory that refers to an employee's belief that good work leads to a specific outcome.

24. **The correct answer is B.** Increased production is the most likely benefit of technological advancements utilized in the workplace. Some technology may improve energy efficiency but not necessarily, so choice C is not the best answer. Technology will have less effect on labor relations and workforce diversity, so choices A and D are incorrect.

25. **The correct answer is B.** Increasing numbers of women in the workforce have brought pay inequity to light and have helped to eliminate jobs that pay men and women differing wages for the same work. The importance of parity in the workforce makes choices A and D incorrect. An increase in the number of immigrants in the workforce has required companies to become more sensitive to diverse backgrounds in their practices and planning, making choice C incorrect.

26. **The correct answer is B.** A short-term time frame and high level of details best describe operational planning. Choice A doesn't make sense as a high level of detail is needed. Choice C describes the characteristics of strategic planning. Choice D describes tactical planning.

27. **The correct answer is A.** An international group of business leaders developed the Caux Principles to address universal business ethics. The main premise of the Caux Principles is showing concern for human dignity and working toward the common good. Global commerce (choice B), accounting standards (choice C), and environmental awareness (choice D) are not the focus of the Caux Principles.

28. **The correct answer is C.** Control systems are established and implemented to help employees behave in the best interests of a business. Control systems, such as performance appraisals and raises, regulate employee performance. A mission statement (choice B) is an organization's basic purpose, but it does not guide employee behavior. Customer organization (choice A) and a tactical plan (choice D) are not specifically geared toward directing the activities of employees.

29. **The correct answer is A.** The Leader-Member Exchange (LMX) theory asserts that group maintenance behaviors, such as trust, mutual respect, mutual loyalty, and open communication, can lead to the development of personal relationships with group members. The LPC theory (choice B) and the Hersey-Blanchard theory (choice D) are situational rather than behavioral leadership theories. Vroom (choice C) is a decision-making situational model that is considered valid for modern management.

30. The correct answer is D. Employee loyalty and cooperation are both potential benefits of a strong organizational culture. Employees who feel like they are members of a team are more likely to remain at a job and work hard. Customer satisfaction (choice A), economic stability (choice B), and ethics enforcement (choice C) are less likely benefits of a strong culture within an organization.

31. The correct answer is A. Top executives make most decisions in centralized organizations. In high-involvement organizations (choice B), upper management seeks a consensus from all levels of the company. In decentralized organizations (choice C), decision-making is dispersed throughout the company. An organization especially skilled at problem solving and creativity is known as a learning organization (choice D).

32. The correct answer is C. Compliance-based ethics programs are designed to impose punishments upon ethics violators. Such programs usually involve increased monitoring of employees and the establishment of legal standards and procedures regarding ethics. In contrast, integrity-based ethics programs attempt to instill a sense of personal responsibility into employees. Choices A, B, and D do not describe compliance-based ethics programs.

33. The correct answer is D. Establishing the mission, vision, and goals of the organization is the first step in the strategic planning process. Analyzing potential opportunities (choice A) is the second stage of the process, and assessing strengths and weaknesses (choice C) is the third stage. Formulating a strategy (choice B) occurs after performing a SWOT analysis in the fourth stage.

34. The correct answer is D. Stretch goals are attainable but demanding goals used by firms to motivate employees to be excellent at their jobs. While stretch goals are challenging and may seem impossible, they are achievable.

35. **The correct answer is B.** A developmental change aims to make an already successful product or service even better. This could be instituted by looking at ways to duplicate the success of one product by creating similar products. An unplanned change (choice A) is usually a reaction to something unexpected or a significant event, such as a natural disaster or the sudden loss of a top executive. A remedial change (choice C) is intended to remedy an issue. A transformational change (choice D) is a radical change that often involves reorganizing a company's management and reporting hierarchy.

36. **The correct answer is D.** Sustainability involves creating a business that can thrive due to its resiliency, economic value, and contributions to the community. This also increasingly involves acting in an environmentally responsible fashion, seeking to utilize natural or green energy when possible and reducing negative environmental impacts. Environmental scanning (choice A) refers to collecting data about various forces in the management environment. Social responsibility (choice B) refers to the idea that corporations have economic, legal, ethical, and philanthropic responsibilities to society. Internal strategies (choice C) are actions taken by businesses to avoid threats and benefit from opportunities.

37. **The correct answer is C.** The accounting department in an automobile manufacturing corporation is a staff department. Staff departments support line departments (choice A), which are the ones responsible for the main activities of a business. A regional department (choice B) is a part of a geographical organization, and a product department (choice D) is a part of a product organization.

38. **The correct answer is C.** When a company's culture creates an environment that hinders its ability to respond to competition or adapt to market changes, it has become problematic. Choices A, B, and D represent the positive effects of a strong corporate culture.

39. **The correct answer is B.** Middle management has been primarily affected by corporate reductions in management staff. Supervisors are needed to directly oversee workers, while CEOs and other top-level managers are needed to guide a company into the future with long-term plans. Middle managers are more expendable in large corporations, such as IBM and Sears, where efficiency and cost effectiveness are becoming extremely important.

40. **The correct answer is D.** Failing to show appreciation for help or failing to compliment employees for working hard are examples of extinction. Positive reinforcement (choice A) involves giving a consequence that encourages a behavior to be repeated. Punishment (choice B) involves an unpleasant consequence, such as criticism or being told to complete an undesirable task. Negative reinforcement (choice C) involves removing an undesirable consequence.

41. **The correct answer is A.** Supply chain management refers to managing an extensive network of facilities and people involved in the process of acquiring raw materials, creating products, and distributing products to customers. Tough competition has increased the need for managers to monitor costs closely at every stage of production and distribution.

42. **The correct answer is C.** With a wide span of control, many workers report to one supervisor. A narrow span of control results in a small number of workers reporting to one supervisor (choice A). In most organizations, workers should report to only one supervisor, so choices B and D are incorrect.

43. **The correct answer is B.** The three types of corporate-level strategies include vertical integration, diversification, and concentration on a single business. Implementation is not a type of strategy.

44. **The correct answer is D.** Technical skills are task-specific. Frontline managers must have strong technical skills because they are directly supervising workers, and problems associated with a task, such as nursing or accounting, arise on a daily basis. Choices A, B, and C are not task-specific knowledge.

45. The correct answer is D. Customers make or break a business. Regulatory agencies (choice A) are an indirect environmental force. Technological innovations (choice B) are an indirect environmental force on the economy in which an organization exists. Competitors (choice C) are a direct environmental force, but not the most critical one.

46. The correct answer is B. Geographic organization is the most common method of departmentalization used by multinational corporations. A geographic organization groups units by geographic areas, such as territories, regions, or countries. The structure is useful when customer needs vary greatly from place to place. Product (choice A), matrix (choice C), and functional (choice D) organizations are less commonly used by multinational corporations.

47. The correct answer is C. The decision by many organizations to outsource jobs to other countries has been driven by low labor costs overseas, as well as an educated work force. For example, firms needing telemarketers often outsource to India where low wages pay for a skilled labor force. Trade agreements (choice A), immigration (choice B), and tax laws (choice D) have less influence on outsourcing than labor costs.

48. The correct answer is D. Vroom developed a situational model of leadership that leads to five possible decision styles. Vroom's model works like a funnel with questions that lead to a recommended decision style. Fayol (choice A) wrote the first theory of management. Fiedler (choice B) developed the least preferred co-worker LPC theory that asserts that a leader's style must match a situation. Maslow (choice C) is known for a hierarchy of motivational needs.

49. The correct answer is C. Porsche has used a differentiation strategy in seeking competitive advantage. Differentiation strategies involve being unique in an industry either through quality, marketing, or service. Walmart is an example of an organization that has used low-cost strategies to gain competitive advantage.

50. **The correct answer is B.** Conceptual skills are needed by top-level managers to understand the objectives and strategies of a business. Determining long-term plans and predicting the benefits or problems associated with mergers, acquisitions, and investments require conceptual skills. A manager needs decision-making (choice A), interpersonal (choice C), and analytical (choice D) skills, but these skills do not relate to long-term strategic planning.

51. **The correct answer is D.** The principle of exception indicates that managers should concentrate on deviations from a standard. Managers save time by paying less attention to cases that are close to an established standard and more attention to exceptions. The principle of exception is an important element of the control process.

52. **The correct answer is C.** Regulators, or regulatory agencies, have the power to investigate business practices. Such agencies include the FAA, EPA, SEC, and OSHA. They monitor business compliance with workplace, product, and environmental safety laws.

53. **The correct answer is B.** Making daily operational decisions is not one of the duties of a board of directors. A board's duties include selecting and evaluating the CEO (choice A), assessing and monitoring a firm' financial performance (choice C), and deciding a firm's strategic direction (choice D).

54. **The correct answer is B.** The leadership role of a manager involves coordinating and directing the activities of workers. Staffing, motivating, and controlling employees and their work are elements of the leadership role. The figurehead role (choice A) refers to a manager's symbolic or ceremonial duties. The monitor role (choice C) involves gathering information that may affect a unit. As a resource allocator (choice D), a manager determines how to distribute money, budget, time, and equipment.

55. **The correct answer is D.** A SWOT analysis is a comparison of the strengths, weaknesses, opportunities, and threats that managers use to formulate strategies. It summarizes the relevant information gathered in the environmental analysis during strategic planning. ABC (choice A) stands for activity-based costing, and CRM (choice B) stands for customer relationship management. An LCA (choice C) is a life-cycle analysis that helps determine the environmental impact of a product.

56. **The correct answer is B.** Societal factors such as birth rate, life expectancy, and immigration affect businesses indirectly. Changes in society affect the work force, which influences how businesses function. Productivity is more closely related to technology issues than societal ones.

57. **The correct answer is A.** The negotiator role involves bargaining with others in an organization to obtain advantages. Managers who negotiate for flexible scheduling or increased salaries are working as negotiators for the benefit of their unit. The liason (choice B) and figurehead (choice C) are both interpersonal roles that involve developing and maintaining good relationships with people. The disseminator role (choice D) relates to providing information to subordinates.

58. **The correct answer is D.** Exchange rates and trade agreements are indirect forces within the global environment. Direct forces (choice B), such as suppliers, have an immediate impact on a business, while indirect forces (choice D) influence a business but not its daily operations. Barriers to entry (choice C) are conditions that prevent new firms from entering an industry, such as distribution channels and government policies.

59. **The correct answer is A.** Recognizing the existence of 10 management roles helps with understanding that every role is connected to another. Choice C is not true because neglecting one or more roles hinders employees from working effectively because each role is equally important. Choices B and D may be true, but they are not related to the 10 roles identified by Mintzberg.

60. **The correct answer is D.** Characteristics of followers and environmental factors are the two situational factors in the path-goal theory. These two factors determine the type of leadership behavior that is most appropriate given the followers and the situation. Motivational methods (choice A), characteristics of leaders (choice B), and leadership style (choice C) are not situational factors in the path-goal theory.

Like what you see? Get unlimited access to Peterson's full catalog of DSST practice tests, instructional videos, flashcards, and more for **75% off the first month!** Go to **www.petersons.com/testprep/dsst** and use coupon code **DSST2020** at checkout. Offer expires July 1, 2021.